10 YEARS A GIRLFRIEND

HOW TO NOT WASTE TIME BEING A GIRLFRIEND IF YOU WANT TO BE A WIFE

Janice Hylton Thompson

Unless otherwise indicated, all scriptures are taken from the King James Version and the New King James Version.

Copyright © 1982 by Thomas Nelson, Inc.
Used by permission. All rights reserved."

{Please note that scriptures in book are highlighted for effect.}

Copyright © 2021
by Janice Hylton-Thompson
All rights reserved.

Cover Designed by Pittershawn Palmer
ankh@creativeankh.com

Edited by Wordwors1

Interior Format by Richa Bargotra

ISBN: 978-1-946242-13-6

Janice Hylton Thompson
P. O. Box 422
Bellville NJ 07109

No part of this book may be reproduced in any form without the written permission of the author, except for brief passages included in a review. However, written permission not needed when quotations are used in church bulletins, orders of service, Sunday school lessons, church newsletters and similar works in the course of Christian instruction or services at a place of Christian worship or other Christian assembly.

Table of Contents

Preface

How I Met & Married My Husband

I met my husband less than one month after my thirty-fourth birthday. I was lying on my bed on my birthday, October 11th, admiring my first published book, *Praying for Our Children.* While I was basking in my glory, the Lord spoke and quickly snapped me back into reality. It's as if a light came on for me, and I had a shocking realization: I was thirty-four years old, still single, with no promising prospects in sight.

Then the Lord spoke and said, *"Get up and get out."* I jumped up quickly and got on my computer to look for activities in and around my community that I could attend. I found a few events, like wine tasting, book signings, financial workshops, and so on.

Most importantly, I found what was called First Fridays. First Fridays is a group of networking entrepreneurs that travel to various cities to hold networking events. Then I remembered that I had a flyer with First Friday's information. I had heard of them and wanted to attend when my book was ready. So that was perfect and right up my alley. It was about a month away, so I jotted it down in my calendar.

In the meantime, I started to go out more. I had brunches in the upper-class community I wanted to live in. Also, I attended a few events at local museums, universities, and libraries. Additionally, I looked for events that were considered "cultured." Many of the men who often attend these events are the type of men I prefer. I prefer cultured, educated, well learned, well-spoken, and of the upper class and men of means.

For the First Friday Networking event, I invited my coworker to attend with me after two of my close church sisters refused the invite. We'll call my coworker Ella. Ella was engaged to be married soon. At the event, Ella was sitting opposite me. Next to Ella was another associate, who we'll call Julia. And across from Julia and next to me was an empty chair.

Well in walks a tall, good-looking, and well-dressed gentleman who recognized Julia. He sat down in the empty chair in front of Julia and next to me. He introduced himself as Michael and started catching up with Julia, with whom he attended high school. Michael was cordial, friendly, made small conversation with us, and exchanged business cards. Michael's card indicated that he was an Executive Vice President at a prestigious organization.

As the evening progressed, I mixed, mingled, and talked to other attendees about my books and exchanged business cards. Back at our table, I texted Ella and told her that I thought Michael was interested in her because he was talking to her a lot. Ella texted back that no, she didn't think Michael liked her. Instead, Ella believed Michael liked me because he followed me with his eyes every time I got up and worked the room.

Michael was an absolute gentleman, kind and generous; he offered us drinks, which we declined. He ordered appetizers for our table and offered us an entrée when the waiter returned. When Ella and I got up to use the restroom, Michael was cordial and helped us with our chairs. When Ella and I went dancing, Michael came over and danced with us.

Later, back at the table, Michael leaned over to me and said, "You must have your mother's legs." Ladies, I caught the cue. And once I caught it, I grabbed it and turned my whole body around to face him while showing a little more leg. I gave Michael my full attention with a flirtatious smile and excitement. I then asked, "So tell me again, where did you say you worked?" He spent the next few minutes telling me about his work, and then he stated that he would love to take me out for dinner.

Ladies, this is called pulling a man in. LOL! Apparently, Michael had been flirting with me all night, but I was missing all the signals! I noticed how well-groomed he was. He was extraordinarily masculine, and OMGOSH, his voice was so sexy with just enough authority and base. I remember he wore a gray sweater, black slacks, a nice blazer, and the cutest circular glasses I have *ever* seen. Those glasses are still my favorite pair after almost eight years of marriage. He even smelled manly, and gosh, he had the nicest teeth.

Furthermore, I noticed how clean his fingernails were and that he had nice hands, soft and big. His shoes were clean and spotless. I had also already noticed how well-spoken he was. Ladies, when I first meet a man, these are some of the things I look for and like in a man. And did I mention how handsome he was? I LOVE A GOOD-LOOKING MAN!

As for me, since the weather was cold and rainy, with a side of sleet, I wore knee-high boots with fishnet stockings and a modest little black dress. My hair was in my favorite style of scrunches waves. It looked like I had a shorter hairstyle. For jewelry, I wore dangling earrings and a charming bracelet to offset the hair. Michael and I talked for the rest of the evening, getting to know a lot about each other. I learned which Church he attended, where he worked, and so on. I also learned that even though he had never been married and had no children, marriage and family were both things he wanted. He also talked a lot about his mom, which I loved.

Ladies, I forgot all about my books and gave Michael my undivided attention for the rest of the evening. He was so intriguing, interesting, and based on what I learned so far; he seemed like the type of man I had been praying to meet. Before the evening ended, Michael said that he would call me to take me out.

Additionally, Michael said that he would get a few copies of my books for his coworkers. I asked if he thought his mom would like to read my book, as he had mentioned that she was an avid reader. When it was time for Ella and me to go home, I hugged Michael and thanked him for being a gentleman and treating us to appetizers.

Michael walked Ella and me to the security desk and watched as we got in our cars and drove off. And I thought to myself, "Oh, I want to talk to him again." Ladies, would you believe it was about a month before Michael contacted me for a date? Guess what I was doing that whole month that he didn't call? I did not call, text, or contact him via social media. Neither did I waste that time wondering why he did not call me to take me out.

Instead, I was busy dating (aka gathering data on other guys and keeping busy with my books.) And about a month later, I posted a few pictures of myself in a lovely suit at an event on Facebook. I commented on my waistline, and Michael jumped into my inbox to ask me if I was praying about my waist. He also asked if he could call me and take me out for drinks that evening. I told him that he could call me in a few hours because I was busy, and I declined to meet up that evening. Many women who have heard my story have asked why I didn't go out with him then. Ladies, it took him a month to make contact; surely you don't think I would jump on the phone right away or agree to go out with him that evening?

When Michael called me later that evening, I talked to him long enough for him to plan a date, seeing I declined to go out for drinks that evening. He asked about dinner the following evening, which was Friday, and I declined. I told him that I had a date. He asked about Saturday, and I told him that I was busy, I had plans. He then asked about brunch on Sunday, and I told him that I already had plans. He inquired about Monday evening, and I agreed after I told him that I would check my calendar. And ladies, that began our journey of dating to marriage.

Monday evening, Michael called to cancel because he was in a business meeting and couldn't get away. He inquired about another day I would be available for dinner. I told him that I would check my calendar and get back to him. Later the same evening, he called and said he wanted to see me and would have the car service drive him. That evening we met up, and before dinner came, Michael asked if he could take me out again the following evening, but I declined. He suggested Wednesday, and I agreed.

On Wednesday at dinner, Michael asked if he could take me out on Thursday, and I declined. He asked about Friday, and I agreed. On Friday night, he again asked if he could take me to breakfast on Saturday, and I accepted because he had to fly out on Sunday morning for a business trip. Two months after our first date, Michael asked to meet my father. At three months, he asked me to be exclusive. But I informed him that I did not do exclusivity and didn't believe in boyfriends and girlfriends.

Michael responded with, "Uh oh." And we still laugh at this almost eight years later. At four months, he told me he loved me, and I said, "Thank you." Also, it was nearly six months before I allowed him to meet my daughter because I don't believe in every man I date, meeting my most precious gift. At six months, Michael wanted to propose but said because I hadn't told him I loved him, he waited.

Why hadn't I told Michael that I loved him? Because I wasn't finished gathering the data, I needed to make an informed decision about him. Why should I say that I loved him if I didn't have all of the information I needed to make an informed decision about him. You see, that's what dating means. Dating means "gathering data so that you can make an informed decision." Dating is also the process of elimination.

Ladies, I am happy to report that Michael proposed months later in October, on my birthday. Furthermore, he wanted us to get married two months later, in December. Two months felt rushed, so we chose instead to get married the following May on Mother's Day Weekend, which is the last weekend before his busy season at work. Ladies, it does not take a man ten years to know if you're the one. My husband says he knew in one month that he was going to marry me. Finally, guess what Michael was doing that whole month before he called me? He watched me on Social Media to see how I acted, behaved and the type of pictures I posted.

Michael said that's why he jumped into my inbox when I posted the photos in that beautiful suit. He wanted to know if I would fit into his life, what kind of woman and mother I was. And if I was someone, he could be proud of and not be embarrassed. As of the publication of *10 Years a Girlfriend*, we have been happily married for almost eight years.

Introduction

Do you want to get married? Do you have a boyfriend? How long have you been waiting for your boyfriend and or baby daddy to marry you? Have you thought that maybe he will never marry you and that you need to pick up your worth and walk away? By the end of *10 Years a Girlfriend,* you will be able to honestly answer these questions.

However, let me warn you that *10 Years a Girlfriend* is NOT for every woman! This book is ONLY for a specific group of women who wants to get married. *10 Years a Girlfriend* is ONLY for women who are tired of the dating insanity and are ready to put in the work to date for marriage only.

Additionally, *10 Years a Girlfriend* is only for women who are done with sacrificing themselves on the altar of boyfriends and wasted time.

Are You one of those women who is finish wasting time being a girlfriend when you want to be a wife? Are you tired of being a girlfriend when you want to be a wife? Let's check your tiredness of being a girlfriend temperature.

Ten Years a Girlfriend is only for women who:

1. Know that you are a wife already.
2. Want to get married without settling.
3. Are tired of being girlfriends.
4. Want to have children ONLY in the covenant of marriage.
5. Are tired of wasting years being girlfriends.

10 Years a Girlfriend is for a new generation of women who have made up in their minds to do things God's Way. Women who are ready to put in the diligence and hard work to walk away from the false meaning of dating.

10 Years a Girlfriend is for women who are ready to take control of:

1. **Your Emotions:** While God created us as emotional beings, it was not His will for us to be controlled and led by our emotions. Instead, God's desire is for us to conquer our emotions because it is our giant.

2. **Your Choices of Men:** A husband is a choice! The man you choose to marry and have babies with will determine the rest of your life. Many of you need to take a serious look in the mirror and ask yourself why you chose the wrong man. And why you continue to have babies with the wrong men.

3. **Your Time:** Make it up in your mind today that you will not waste another second with a dead situation. Beginning today, you will not waste any more time being a girlfriend when you want to be a wife. It's time for you to pick up your worth and walk!

4. **Your Cookies aka Pretty Kitty:** Why do you dish the cookie/pretty kitty out like government cheese? Why do you allow every man to pet your pretty kitty?

5. **Your Womb:** Your womb is your Fort Knox that should be protected at all cost. Only your husband should have access to your womb. Your womb is your Holy Grail. Do you know how valuable your womb is?

6. **Your Eggs:** Ladies, we have a Gold Mine between our thighs. Like our womb, our eggs are the Holy Grail. So, take control

of your ability to procreate. Take control of your vagina, aka cookies, aka pretty kitty.

Ladies, you get to choose the father of your children. Please tell me why many women continue to have babies with bums, fixer-uppers, and criminals? Also, why continue to have babies with men who have not married you?

7. **Your Life**: You get to choose the type of life you want to have. The man you choose will determine the rest of your life, so please choose your path wisely. Of course, I am not talking about circumstances you do not have control over. I am speaking strictly in the context of dating and marriage.

I pray that *10 Years a Girlfriend* will cause a stirring in the hearts of my single sisters who want to get married but are settling for girlfriend status. How many of you want to get married but are settling for girlfriend status? How many of my sisters in the Lord attend Church every Sunday, Bible studies, and Sunday school who have settled for being a girlfriend, but you want to get married?

Additionally, how many professional and brilliant women do you know that should know better but are settling for girlfriend and baby mama status? Again, these are women who want to get married but are settling for being girlfriends.

I am also amazed that so many women are settling for side-chick status. Think about it, in your circle of friends, family, coworkers, how many ladies do you know who are wasting time waiting for their boyfriends and baby daddies to marry them?

Finally, how many boyfriends and baby daddies eventually shattered the dreams of their faithful girlfriends and baby mamas and married other women in less than a year?

STOP IT, LADIES, PICK UP YOUR WORTH AND WALK!!

All Your Boyfriends

Before we jump into *10 Years a Girlfriend*, let's do the Boyfriend Check Test. Have some boyfriends become husbands? Sure. Have some boyfriends dated their girlfriends for years and then married them? Absolutely. Have there been college sweethearts that dated and then got married years afterward? Yes.

However, did you know that most boyfriends do not become husbands? Ladies let's look at all of your boyfriends to see how they worked out for you. Prayerfully, this will help you to realize that you need to STOP BEING GIRLFRIENDS if you want to be a wife! Please answer the following:

1. How old are you?
2. How many boyfriends have you had?
3. How many kids do you have out of wedlock?
4. How many baby daddies do you have?
5. How many of those men asked you to marry them?
6. How many men have you shacked up with, and for how long?
7. How many of them married you?
8. How many boyfriends broke your heart?
9. How many years have you wasted with boyfriends?

Now think about your close friends and families and answer these questions for them. Finally, if you want to get married, how is it going for you? How has having multiple boyfriends worked out for you? Prayerfully, when you've completed this book, you will decide to say NO MORE BOYFRIENDS!!

How to NOT Give Boyfriends Husband Benefits

As the old folks would say, *"why should a man buy the whole cow when he's getting the milk for free?"* Updated to the 21st century; *"don't give boyfriends, husbands benefits."* I am amazed at the number of women who frown upon not giving boyfriends, husbands benefits. But then again, many women have wasted years giving away the milk for free even though they want to get married. What does 'don't give boyfriends husband benefits' really mean?

Husband benefits are given in the covenant of marriage to your husband. And should not be given to boyfriends, ever! Neither are they to be given to the men you date. Why? Because boyfriends are temporary, and dating is ONLY to collect data to make an informed decision. Dating is not about sex, babies, shacking up, and so on. The following are seven benefits that should ONLY be given to a husband and not a boyfriend. Because husbands have put in the work to provide, protect, and profess. Thus, he has earned these benefits.

1. Your Body: The first benefit is your body, which is God's temple. My body being the temple of God, was one of the revelations I got when I was younger and single. To understand that your body is the temple of God, please read about King Solomon's Temple. You can read it in First Kings and Second Chronicles. I am still in awe every time I read about King Solomon's Temple. When reading about the tabernacle in the old testament, it had three major parts:

a. **Outer Court or The Courtyard**
b. **Inner Court or The Holy Place**
c. **Holy of Holies or The Most Holy Place**

The outer court was where the priest got the offerings ready. The Inner Court was where the altar of incense, showbread, and lampstands were. But the Holy of Holies or The Most Holy Place is where The Ark of the Covenant and God's glory abided.

In the Ark of the Covenant was: The Ten Commandments, Aaron's Rod that budded, and a bowl of Manna. The Most Holy Place could only be entered once per year on the Day of Atonement by one man: The High Priest. The High Priest's purpose was to spread sacrificial blood on the altar to atone for the people's sins.

The Hight Priest going into The Most Holy Place is also referred to as going beyond the veil. In the Tabernacle example, I applied its concept to my body. I understood that my body should only be entered by my high priest—my husband, who paid the price of marriage to have me in his life. My husband went through the process to profess his love, provide for, and protect me.

2. Children: The second benefit that you should never give a boyfriend is children. The first command God gave to Adam and Eve in **Genesis 1:28** was to be fruitful and multiply. Therefore, that tells me that we should only have children in the bonds and covenant of marriage. I had my daughter Alexia when I was sixteen years old. Please don't get upset because I said we should only have babies in marriage.

The Bible also mentions, in **Proverbs 13:22,** that a good man leaves an inheritance for his children's children. God has also charged parents in **Proverbs 22:6** to train our children in the way they should go. Therefore, as parents, we are to be examples for our children to follow. Now, please don't go getting emotional and angry. The Bible is right whether we like it or not. Many of us, including myself, have had children outside of marriage's covenant. Our children are still blessed and favored by God. However, God desires that we turn from our ways and turn to His way of doing things.

3. The Comforts of Living Together: The third benefit you should never give a boyfriend is the comforts of living together. When God brought Eve to Adam, he was an already made and prepared man. Adam had a job and a home. Adam was able to provide for and protect a wife and children. Adam was not trying to move in with Eve. Lol! God said it was not good for man to be alone. God created Eve and held a whole wedding ceremony for Adam and Eve. By reading the Bible, there are tons of examples of couples getting and being given into marriage. However, the only example of anyone shacking up is the Samaritan woman, and Jesus was not pleased with her.

4. Submission: The fourth benefit women should never give a boyfriend is the blessing of submission. If I hear another single woman talk about submitting to their boyfriends, I am going to scream!! Submission is for husbands ONLY! The Bible says in **Ephesians 5: 21 Submitting yourselves one to another in the fear of God. [22] Wives, submit yourselves unto your own husbands, as unto the Lord. [23] For the husband is the head of the wife, even as Christ is the head of the church: and he is the saviour of the body. [24] Therefore as the church is subject unto Christ, so let the wives be to their own husbands in every thing. [25] Husbands, love your wives, even as Christ also loved the church, and gave himself for it; [26] That he might sanctify and cleanse it with the washing of water by the word...**

For the naysayers and angry group of women with Jezebel spirits, who hate men, fathers, husbands, God, and the Bible, submission is not a bad thing. It is vital to understand that a wife submitting to her husband is a picture of the Church submitting to Christ. Additionally, understanding that marriage is a picture of the union between Christ and the Church is essential. Also, any situation where a wife is being abused or mistreated under the guise of "submission" is not biblical and godly submission. Abuse and mistreatment are NOT examples of how Christ treats the Church. Christ Loves the Church!

What does submission mean? Submission means to come under another authority. For example, the Church is under the authority of Christ. Christ is head of the Church. In other words, submission means to go under the vision of another. So, ladies, make sure you can submit to the vision of that man you love so much and want to marry. Sisters, I encourage you to choose the vision you will submit to wisely.

One of the reasons there is so much stress, and drama in marriages is because many women marry men who had no vision. And those wives are trying to get their husbands to submit to their vision. A visionless man has no vision for his marriage and family, which causes the marriage to be a struggling one.

5. Access: The fifth husband benefit you should not give to boyfriends is access. I am shocked at the number of women who buy homes, have joint bank accounts, and begin businesses with their boyfriends. I have heard of foolish women who take out life insurance policies and make their boyfriends their beneficiaries. And the newest foolery is starting YouTube channels with their boyfriends. Why?

Yet these same boyfriends have not married their foolish girlfriends, and it's crazy!! The sad thing is that many of these women are trying to prove their love to their boyfriends, hoping they will marry them. Please stop the madness, ladies! If a man doesn't value you enough to make you his wife, why begin a life with him?

6. Love: Sixth in the not giving boyfriends, husbands benefits is Love. The book of **Ephesians 5:25** admonishes the husband to love his wife like Christ loves the Church. Yet, many girlfriends love their boyfriends more than their boyfriends love them. Many girlfriends work several jobs to keep their boyfriends happy because they "love" their boyfriends so much. And their boyfriends want to be kept, men.

Ladies, please stop falling in love and loving every man you meet. Your heart was not created to be broken by man after man. Get some discipline and learn to date for marriage only. Please be sure to pick up my other book, *23 Types of Guys You Might Meet.* It will revolutionize your dating life, journey and teach you about the various types of guys you might meet. Additionally, it will teach you how to vet the guys you meet correctly.

7. Spoiled: The seventh and final benefit you should not give to boyfriends is spoiling them. I have heard woman after woman spoiling their boyfriends and buying them heaven and earth. Recently one lady bought her boyfriend an investment property, but he got upset that she did not buy him a Rolex watch instead. The crazy thing is, she recorded it and posted it on social media, and everyone went in on her. Guess what she did? She defended her boyfriend while he sat there and said nothing. She claimed she was spoiling her boyfriend by buying him an investment property.

The above example is what I mean about a visionless man. She has a vision that her boyfriend does not have. However, she is trying to get him to have her vision. No, his vision was a Rolex watch. Her boyfriend that she wanted to spoil vision was not an investment property, which would enable him to begin building wealth. Did I mention he was her "BOYFRIEND!?"

Ladies, trying to get your boyfriend to have your vision because he doesn't have one is nothing more than throwing your pearls in front of swine. That foolish man did not have the vision his foolish girlfriend had. And she was trying to get him to have her vision, but his vision was a Rolex watch. BOTH FOOLISH!!

The Tale of Two Wives and a Girlfriend

There have been so many males who have talked about women who want to get married. Those males told those poor foolish women that they don't need that 'lil' piece of government sanction paper to prove that they love each other.

The Tale of Two Wives is two testimonials from my book *The Naked Wife*. Two wives who didn't walk away empty-handed because they got the 'lil' piece of paper. Additionally, it is the story of a very foolish thirty-one-year-old girlfriend who has decided to waste almost ten years of her life waiting on her boyfriend to be ready to marry her.

Wife #1 was married for ten years. She worked two jobs while her husband was finishing medical school. She paid all living expenses, bought them a house, and paid for family and kids' expenses. Once her husband completed medical school and started to work, he decided that he didn't love his wife anymore. Wife #1 was shocked and hurt, but she pulled herself together and decided that she did not want to stay with a man who didn't love her. So, she came up with a plan and quit her job to go back to school. In divorce court, the judge gave her alimony, child support, the house, and savings.

Wife #1 husband told the judge that she had a good job, but she quit it to go back to school. The judge asked him who was taking care of him all those years. Wife #1 said that she received more in alimony per month in the divorce settlement than she earned as a teacher. Congratulations to her, right?

Question: how many women do you know, or have you heard of that shacked up for years with their boyfriends and or baby daddies that they had absolutely nothing to show for it? Many women must start from scratch to build a life after all of those wasted years.

These women also waste years of their lives with boyfriends waiting for them to marry them. Afterward, they must try to meet someone new when they are older, making dating and settling down trickier. Please do not think that this is only about money and what we can get when a marriage is over. Ladies, what about all the wasted time, effort, and energy?

Wife #2 went to see a lawyer after about eight years of marriage. You see, her husband could not keep his dingaling in his pants. The Lawyer requested that she provided all their financial documents. After the lawyer reviewed the records, he asked if her husband was abusing her. Wife #2 said no. Their only issue is cheating. The lawyer told her to go home, make her husband a nice dinner, and stay with him for two more years. That would make it ten years. After ten years of marriage, she would be entitled to half of everything they had. Wife #2 followed the lawyer's advice and waited an additional two years to file for divorce.

When Wife #2 left her cheating husband, she went with a lifetime of benefits and alimony. Ladies, how many women do you know who shacked up for ten years and walked out of the relationship with nothing to show for all of those wasted years? Why waste time building a life on sand instead of on a firm, rock foundation?

Finally, I had an interaction with a young woman who was thirty-one years old. I will refer to her as a foolish girlfriend. Foolish Girlfriend's boyfriend was twenty-seven, and they had been dating and shacking up for three years. Foolish Girlfriend was ready to get married, but her boyfriend was not ready. Foolish Girlfriend asked her boyfriend when would he be ready to get married, and he said in eight years.

Would you believe that the thirty-one years old foolish girlfriend decided to wait for her twenty-seven-year-old boyfriend to be ready to marry her in eight years? I was floored when she said she would wait. I tried my best to reason with her that her boyfriend did not want to marry her. He was saying he will be ready in eight years in hopes that she would move along.

Additionally, I tried to talk to her about her age and that at thirty-five, women are automatically considered high-risk when it comes to having children. Her boyfriend waiting eight years to get married and begin a family, would land her at thirty-nine years old.

Furthermore, I asked what if her boyfriend decided that he did not want to marry her after eight years? Because reading between the lines, he did not say he would be ready to marry her. Instead, he said he would be prepared to get married in eight years. Who is to say he will marry *her*?

Unfortunately, she was adamant that her boyfriend would marry her in eight years. Recently, Foolish Girlfriend posted on social media that she is ready to have children. But unfortunately, her boyfriend, who she is waiting on to marry her, is not ready to start a family yet. Foolish Girlfriend asked if she should just go ahead and get pregnant. She is now thirty-four years old at the publication of *10 Years a Girlfriend.*

Why Dating is NOT What You Thought

Dating one guy at a time is like going to college and taking one course per semester! Let's assume the number of credits required for you to obtain a degree is seventy. How many of you know that it would take you forever to complete the requirements to attain your degree? Unfortunately, many women date like the above example of taking one course per semester.

Likewise, many women do not understand the true meaning of dating. Dating is not about meeting a man and committing to him. Dating is not making a man you just met your "boyfriend." Dating is not about having sex, shacking up, and making babies out of marriage. Dating is not making a home with a man you are not married to.

Dating, however, is about gathering data or information about men so that you can make an informed decision about them. Dating is also the process of elimination. Why is dating also the process of elimination? Because there are some men you will date who you will need to eliminate or stop dating. Why? Because based on the data you gathered, you learn that they are not what you want in a husband. No wasted time, drop them and move on. Remember, dating is about gathering data so that you can make an informed decision! A man is not your man; he is just a prospect.

Therefore, for you to properly date, you need to know what you want in a husband. And if you begin to date a man and you learn that he is not what you want, you need to quickly eliminate him from your list of prospects and move on to dating other men. Remember, dating is about gathering data so that you can make an informed decision.

So, if dating is about gathering data, why do you need to commit to the stranger you just met? Furthermore, if dating is about gathering data, why not collect data on more than one guy at a time? One main factor that I notice single women faces is that many don't date.

Many of my single sisters meet a man and automatically make that man their man and commit to him without knowing who he is. Many women shack up, have babies, and make permanent decisions with temporary men. Most women do not date in the true meaning of dating to determine if a man is right for them based on what they want in a husband.

Several women are in long-term situationships, wasting years for their boyfriends or baby daddies to marry them. How can we fix this craziness? Sadly, many women were not taught how to choose a husband wisely by dating different men. What is dating again?

Growing up in the Church, I remember hearing the following: *"Christians don't date."* Puzzled and in disbelief would be an understatement of how I felt because, in my twenty-something mind, that made no sense. Here's an example of how data works. When I was in school, while researching various topics, the professors instructed us to gather our data so that we could write a concise paper on our thesis.

So, to me, dating meant gathering information. I believe that the Church has done many singles a disservice on how they taught about dating and marriage. For example, when I was an adolescent, there was a book about saying goodbye to dating. I tried reading it because all churches were pushing for young singles to read it.

However, I could not read it because I felt the Holy Spirit impressing on my heart that it was wrong for me. A few years back, when I wrote my dating book, *23 Types of Guys You Might Meet*, I tried to read that book about saying goodbye to dating. I just could not read the book; it was as if the Holy Spirit would not allow me to. Let me remind you that I am an avid reader! I read all types of books, so for me, not being able to read that book was shocking. From what I was told, the book's view of dating is fornication, having babies out of wedlock, shacking up, and so on.

Therefore, to avoid all those sinful acts, many churches were pushing for singles, not to date. Additionally, the Church had a statement that never sat right with me. They would say, *"Christians don't date."* However, my idea of dating was about a thousand degrees opposite their dating view.

So the "church" believed that singles in the Church should not date.

Why? Because their concept of dating is sexual immoralities, shacking up, and having babies out of wedlock. Unfortunately, what not dating, aka gathering data, has resulted in is many single women in the Church having boyfriends. Many single women meet one man and make them their men.

And sadly, these poor women have wasted years waiting for their boyfriends to get ready to marry them. This mindset has also caused many churches to be filled with single women and single mothers. Also, many just meet a man and get married without gathering the data they needed to make an informed decision.

I thought the Church's dating concept was crazy because when I hear the word dating, I hear data, aka information. Again, as mentioned earlier, dating is not about sex, shacking up, or having babies out of wedlock. However, dating is gathering DATA about a man to make an informed decision about him. Dating is also the process of elimination.

Here's an example of me eliminating a man interested in me. I was 19 years old, and a young man I attended school with showed up at my Church. He wanted to talk to my father in the faith about marrying me.

My father had a rule of not talking to anyone after Church on Sundays because he was tired from preaching. So, my father told me to go to dinner with the young man and pay attention to how he treated me. By the time dinner was over, I knew that I did not want to go out with him again.

This young man was beautifully saved and a young minister in training. We were both born again, but I knew I did not want to go out with him again because of the data I gathered on him. Neither did I want to marry him or waste one second trying to fix him.

23 Types of Guys You Might Meet

To make sure you get a good understanding of what dating is, here's an excerpt from my book, *23 Types of Guys You Might Meet*. If you have not read that book, you must. It is a powerhouse of dating wisdom and resources. You might think this information is redundant, but please understand that I want to make sure you have a grounded understanding of what DATING REALLY IS.

Portions from my book *23 Types of Guys You Might Meet*: Dating is about gathering data or information so that you can make an informed decision about men. Dating is also the process of elimination. Gathering data can also be considered as vetting a man. In other words, you meet a guy or several guys, and you are to gather information or data about them so that you can make an informed decision about them. Twenty years ago, we only had home phones and beepers.

Today, we have smartphones, social media, and various ways to communicate. Many churches were against "dating" when I was younger. Many in the Church would often say, "Christians don't date." As a young woman who always wanted to get married, I was confused by this. I never understood how we were to meet a potential mate, get to know them and decide if we want to marry them without dating, aka getting information on them. Could that be one reason why the divorce rate is about 51% in the Church? However, the divorce rate is steady at 50% in the world.

In the past, people were getting married only because they were saved. However, many did not have things in common, and, sometimes, they didn't even like each other. Some saints make the mistake of thinking that if two people are saved, they can get married and make it work! That is a lie from the pits of hell! In some churches, the belief is that God will send us the perfect mate so that we could marry them. There was no need to get to know one another because God sent them, meaning they must be right. I am incredibly picky, and I had a good idea of the type of husband I desired. I wasn't going to up and marry some man just because we were both saved.

However, my concern was that I wasn't meeting the type of man I would want to marry. And since the teaching in many churches was that being saved was all a couple needed to get married. The Church's method of meeting a man and going straight to the altar was going to leave me single forever. Many brothers expressed interest in me, but I refused to even go out with most of them. I needed a man to be more than saved because I wanted to have things in common with my husband.

Additionally, financial security was a must because I hate lack and debt, and I am allergic to struggling through life. However, as I got older and studied for myself, I have learned that "dating" means merely gathering data or information about a person. When done correctly, dating has nothing to do with sex, shacking up, having babies out of wedlock, taking care of a man, or anything against the Word of the Lord.

Dating is for the simple purpose of gathering information about a potential partner. Some churches teach us that God will send your husband to the Church, and then you two will get married. That mindset has confused many Christian women and has resulted in many remaining single, waiting for their Boaz to come and find them at the Church. Sadly, many women feel that they are to be loyal and automatically commit to a man they just met.

As a result, these women refuse to date, aka gather data, on many men. Why? Because they believe they are in a relationship and need to be faithful to this man, they just met. That doesn't make any sense. If you meet a young man you are getting to know, why would you be committed to him when you just met and don't know him?

Would You "Date" Three Guys at One Time?

The following is an excerpt from my book *23 Types of Guys You Might Meet*. Ladies, please stop meeting one man and make him the ONE. Please discipline yourself to gather data on the men you meet according to what you want in a husband.

Gathering data will enable you to choose your husband accordingly to what you want in your husband. I have dated quite a few guys in my single days. I have another book coming soon about several guys I dated. However, only my husband fit my list of what I wanted in a husband. Do you remember what dating is? Exactly! So, date accordingly and choose your husband wisely.

All the stories included in *10 Years a Girlfriend* are of women who met one man, set their eyes on him, and thought they would make the men marry them. Many are still waiting after twenty and thirty years for the men to value them enough to marry them. But what if these women and perhaps you who are reading *10 Years a Girlfriend* dated accordingly?

From 23 Types of Guys You Might Meet:

Here's a question I post to many of my Christian sisters: "If you meet three guys in one week who want to take you out, who would you go out with?" They all said they would go out with the first guy and forget about the other two because to do otherwise would be cheating. But how is that cheating? You are not courting, engaged, or married to the guy you just met yesterday. How is going out for coffee with guys #2 and #3 cheating?

How can you assume that guy #1 is your "Boaz"? How do you automatically decide that this guy you just met and know absolutely nothing about is your husband? The crazy thing that I see many women do is automatically commit to being in a relationship with guy #1 without getting to know him first or getting any information about him.

The problem comes when he's not the man she needs. What if he doesn't attend church or believe in giving tithes and offerings? Maybe he doesn't think that a husband is to provide for his wife and family. Sadly, instead of walking away, many women try to turn guy #1 into the man they need. You are committing to men without having the proper information to make an informed decision.

Committing without data has resulted in many divorces, not only in our churches but in our nation, in my opinion. This, my dear, is the dilemma that many sisters are in. I will be writing more extensively about dating soon, but for now, please be informed that it is okay to DATE and GATHER DATA on guys who show interest in you.

So, if you meet three brothers in a week that all want to take you out, you at least need to talk with all of them so you can gather data about them to see if you have things in common. You should not meet a guy and automatically jump into a relationship with him and begin to plan a wedding with this man you don't know.

Now, there are a few instances when people have met, and they both knew they were meant for each other. However, that's not the norm. Therefore, it is essential to gather data on potential mates to get to know which one is your "ONE."

What if you refused to go out with or at least talk to guy #2 and #3 for guy #1, and come to find out that he doesn't even want to get married? Now the other two are gone because you automatically thought guy #1 was your Boaz. Or what if you fell head-over-heels in love with guy #1, and he doesn't feel the same way about you?

But guy #1 strings you along for five years because he needs to live off you, saying he's going to marry you. Some men will also go as far as giving you a "shut-up ring." Ladies, you don't want to force a man to marry you. You are a gift and a prized possession. You should be treated as a special gift for your husband.

Where are Your Marital Hopes?

Does the following scenario sound familiar? You meet the most wonderful guy, and you set your eyes, heart, mind, and soul on him. You make him your prize and claim him to be your husband. You have made up in your mind that you will make him marry you because you love him and want him to be your baby's daddy and husband.

So, stepping out on faith, you claimed him as your husband. And you placed all your marital hopes and dreams in his flimsy, possibly full of holes, basket. It doesn't matter how long it takes or what you must do; you are going to nag him, wash, cook, clean, sex him, pop babies out for him until he marries you.

Year after year, you continue to play the role of wife, and next thing you know, it's been ten years. To date, he hasn't mentioned marrying you, much less proposing. But you're in so deep, and you feel stuck. Though you want to get married, what do you do after years of being with this man who hasn't married you? Together you build the American dream of a home, kids, dogs, and the white picket fence.

Why hasn't he married you? You have been his counselor, peace, and his soft place to land on. You washed, cooked, cleaned, had sex with him in every which way he desires, and, to date, technically, you're still single. Sister, I'm sorry to tell you, but you are caught up in the forever girlfriend web of deception and unrealistic expectations!

Unfortunately for many girlfriends, their faithful boyfriends later left them and married another chick he met six months ago. "Allegedly," he wasted your time, hurt you, whispered sweet lies, and sold you a bag of dreams. He left you with broken promises, stressed you out over the years, and has your boobs and kitty sagging from his five big head kids.

Ladies, God established marriage in Genesis by marrying Adam and Eve. Marriage is the will of God for us, and not shacking up and popping babies out for males who have not married us. Yet, many of us, especially those who want to get married, continue to fall into wasting years waiting for boyfriends to marry us.

So how can you fix this? I am so glad you asked. Beginning today, take a step of faith and commit to stop committing to men who haven't put a ring on it. If you want to get married, stop wasting time with men who don't want to marry you. Learn to date, drop, and move on.

Dating and dropping men who do not match up to what you want in a husband is easy. Why? Because you made no commitments to them. You didn't allow yourself to get emotionally involved. Therefore, you have nothing to be disappointed about. You did not make a family to break up.

Therefore, you can move on with your head held high because you did not put all of your marital hopes and dreams in a man's flimsy, possibly full of holes basket.

The Dating Insanity Web of Entanglements

As mentioned in the previous chapter, dating, or gathering data on one guy at a time is like going to college and taking one course per semester! Not surprisingly, dating for marriage for many single women is like the above example. Therefore, dating several guys at a time to choose the best husband is a foreign concept to many single women.

Women grow up going from one boyfriend to another vs. dating for marriage. And if a man is not marriage material, dropping him and moving on is unheard of. Many women date or gather data on one guy at a time and hope that he will marry them, even if that guy is not suitable for them.

Ladies, the INSANITY of dating the same old way will only get you the same old results you've obtained for years. Used up, popping several babies out of wedlock for every man you lay with and years of wasted time. Finally, your precious boyfriends will almost overwhelmingly eventually leave you and marry other women in about a year.

Why? Because they love those women and want to marry, provide for, and protect them, not you! How many of you who have been caught up in the dating web of dating insanity realize that you need to begin to DATE DIFFERENTLY?

Again, what is dating? Dating is simply the art of skillfully gathering data or information on men to make an informed decision about them. Dating is also the process of elimination. Therefore, if you meet a man and there is a mutual interest, you can begin the process of data gathering. If you learn something about him that is not according to what you want in a husband; you need to eliminate him from your dating portfolio and move on.

Unfortunately, many women find data gathering on multiple guys strenuous. Do you know why? Because most women meet a guy and make him their man, without knowing anything about him. And that's being lazy! Thus, causing you to develop emotional attachments. And having emotional attachments and commitments makes it difficult to walkway.

Many women meet men and begin to build a life with them without gathering data. For example, many women have several babies, moving in together, and putting all their marital hopes and dreams in one man's possible full of holes, flimsy basket.

My sisters, it is so crucial for you to learn to date without committing to the men you date and not develop emotional attachments. Committing to men without dating, aka gathering data, is the number one mistake most women make, in my opinion.

How Long Does It Take for Men to Know if You're the One?

One of the questions I get asked a lot is, how long does it take for a man to know if you are the one or not? Well, my father and many other men have told me that a man knows by three months. So, if you've been with your boyfriend for ten years, he knew nine years and nine months ago that you are not the one for him.

In other words, it could be the same day, a week later, or in a month or two. But men know by three months if you're their wife or not. Not three, thirteen, or twenty years, but men **KNOW BY THREE MONTHS IF THEY WANT TO MARRY YOU!** Isn't that exciting, ladies? My husband said he knew in one month that he would marry me. After it took him a month to call me and plan a date, he said he knew he would marry me on our first date. Surprisingly, I felt that I would marry him in about a month or so. How did I know? Read on.

Unfortunately, there is a downside to this information, ladies. And that is when you have been "dating" a man for six years, and he says he is not ready to get married. Truthfully, he is letting you know that you are not the one. When most men say they do not want to get married, what they mean is that they do not want to marry you.

You see, the 'you' is silent. Ladies, please keep this in mind when you continue to waste year after year waiting for your long-term boyfriends to marry you. They are wasting your time while they try to find the ONE! Have some boyfriends told their girlfriends that they were not ready to get married and do not want to marry but end up marrying those same ladies? Yes—however, that is not the norm.

Many men who say they are not ready to get married or do not want to get married often end up meeting THEIR ONE and marry them in months. I had a baby at sixteen because I was not adequately taught about sex and marriage. I am so thankful that my father in the faith pulled me to the side and told me not to have any more kids out of wedlock if I wanted to get a good husband.

Not only did I listen, but I also implemented his fatherly advice. Thus, both of my kids are twenty years apart. And I had my son as a married woman. At the publication of *10 Years a Girlfriend*, I am 43 years old, with a 26-year-old and a six-year-old. My husband and I are also believing the Lord for another baby.

Let me tell you; I was a better mom at 37 when I had my son than I was at sixteen when I had my daughter. From 17 years old until I met my husband at 34, I made up in my mind that I was a wife, and I wanted a husband. I wanted a husband, not a boyfriend, friend with benefits, baby daddy, or a sugar daddy.

I wanted a husband that could profess his love to me, provide a good life for my daughter and me, and protect us. I refused to settle for anything lesser than what God planned for me. During my singleness, I took time to renew my mind, studied God's Word, prayed, and fasted, and worked tirelessly on what I wanted in a husband.

Ladies, renewing your mind from being a girlfriend to wife takes hard work, sacrifice, dedication, and diligence. Now, are kids going to say they have boyfriends and girlfriends? Of course, they are but continue to plant the seed of the covenant of marriage to them. Tell them God's plan for them is the blessed covenant of marriage. Not shacking up, having multiple kids out of wedlock, and wasting time with tons of males who just want to use them for their bodies.

Most importantly, when it comes to your children, please be sure to have the communication doors open. This way, your babies can come and talk to you about everything and anything.

How Long Have You Been Waiting for Your Boyfriend to Marry You?

I am amazed at the number of women who have wasted years of their lives waiting for their boyfriends or baby daddies to marry them. *10 Years a Girlfriend* is a snapshot of some everyday women wasting time waiting for their boyfriends and or baby daddies to marry them.

I conducted a quick survey with a few ladies about how long they

have been waiting for their boyfriends to marry them. Here's what I found.

Question: *how long have you been waiting for your boyfriend to marry you?*

- Eight years together, two babies and another on the way, and still no ring.
- Nine years, dating since I was nineteen; he was 46 and still no ring.
- Ten years dating, and I know that he plans to propose, so I'm just waiting.
- Thirteen years, five kids, and I have been wondering if he will ever marry me.
- Fourteen years with a break at year ten, and still no ring.
- Fourteen years and pregnant again. Hopefully, this baby is a boy, and he'll go ahead and marry me.
- Fifteen years, three beautiful kids, and still waiting.
- Twenty years, started as high school sweethearts and no ring or even talks of getting married.

- Twenty years plus everything that a married couple needs to build a life together, except we are not married.
- He was my first boyfriend at fourteen, and fifteen years later, I'm still waiting for him to marry me.
- Twenty years with my boyfriend, and still hoping he will propose.

Ladies, I don't know about you, but those few testimonials are disturbing. My dear sister, if you are not careful, you will end up wasting ten years of your life waiting for your boyfriend or baby daddy to marry you.

The truth is that you might not be his ONE. You might not be the woman he wants to die for. Yes, I said, "*die for.*" You see, a husband must "*die*" for his wife. I will be writing more extensively about this soon, so please look out for that book.

You see, there have been women who have been waiting years for their boyfriend to marry them. I hope that if you find yourself in any of these examples, *10 Years a Girlfriend* will Empower you to pick up your worth and walk. You are worth more than wasting your life with *10 Years a Girlfriend.*

There is a man out there who will love you and wants to marry you.

The following stories range from one year a girlfriend to forty-five years. Can you imagine waiting forty-five years for a man to marry you? I imagine you said no. I couldn't imagine it either, but one year becomes two years, and the next thing you know, it's been twenty years.

1 Year a Girlfriend

Heart on the Outside

I've been dating this sweet guy for a few months now. Every time we speak, I get butterflies. I just want to spend all day and night talking to him. I was hoping that he would take me out, but instead, he broke it off with me. When I asked him why he broke up with me when he hasn't even taken me out yet, he said he just doesn't feel the same way about me that I do about him. Looking back now, I initiated a lot. And I wore my heart on my sleeve because I thought if I just let him know how much I cared, he would care about me too.

First Date Cookies

Thinking back now, I guess it was foolish of me to sleep with my boyfriend of three months on the first date. He said it was not an issue, especially since we got busy every time we saw each other. I cannot help but think that's why he ghosted me.

Why Guys Ghost Us

I do not understand why guys ghost us for the life of me. After four months of talking, texting, we went on two dates, and then he ghosted me. It just makes no sense to me. We had a great time and enjoyed each's other company. The least he could have done was give me closure. To us up and ghost me like that? That's so childish of him.

Kiss My Feet

A dirty, lowlife dog is what my boyfriend of 6 months is. I cooked for him and cleaned his home. I even kissed his funky feet for his 30th birthday. And what did I get? Dumped!

He Said I was Boring

I dated my boyfriend for almost a year, only for him to break up with me. He said I was boring. Boring? What does that mean? I was looking forward to a ring because I thought things were going so well with us.

Make Me Exclusive or Else

My boyfriend and I have been together for almost a year. I told him that it was time for us to be exclusive, and he said he does not believe in exclusivity. So, I told him that if he did not make me exclusive, we might as well go our separate ways. Can you believe he said, "ok?" I thought things were going well for us. How can he throw us away so easily?

Happy Anniversary

I've been dating online because of COVID-19. I met this guy on one of the dating apps, and we've been chatting going on three months. Surprisingly, I've developed feelings for him even though we haven't met in person yet. A few days ago, while having one of our late-night conversations, he said he would send me flowers for our three-month anniversary. Three days later, and no flowers. I've been asking him about the flowers he promised me, and he said he's been busy but promised me that he would order them. So, I asked him about the flowers a few days later and would you believe that he blocked me.

My Credit is Messed Up

My boyfriend moved in with me two weeks after we met. He wasn't working, but I saw potential in him. So, I helped him with his resume and to find a job. Also, he didn't have any credit, so I added him to my credit card. And I helped him get a car on my credit and paid the down payment for him.

The relationship got crazy because we were fighting every day.

The fights were mainly because he wanted to stay out all night and come home two and three in the mornings. So, he moved out and moved in with a new girl who is putting up with his crap. Now I'm trying to get the car back because my credit is messed up. He is not paying for the vehicle like he said he would. The crazy thing is, I thought he was the one for me.

Three Boyfriends in One Year

I don't know what else to do. I've had three boyfriends this year, and after a few months, they all just don't want to be bothered with me. All my boyfriends have been like that over the years. Most of them ghost me, and I never hear from them again. I'm starting to think that something is wrong with me.

I Told Them I Wanted to Get Married

Every guy I started to date said that they are not ready for a serious relationship. The last two guys I dated were for two years each, even though, from the beginning, I had made it clear to them that I want to get married. I was just hoping that they would change their minds and marry me.

Single Mother Choice

I am three months pregnant for my boyfriend of five months. He wanted me to get rid of the baby because he is not ready to be a father. Plus, he said it might not be his because I was "out there." Also, he told me that if I chose to have the baby, I would be a single mom, and he would not want anything to do with the baby. And to think I was thinking I wanted us to get married? SMH!

Break Time

I've been seeing this guy for a whole year. He said he likes it when women come over to wash, cook and clean his apartment for him. So, for the last year, every week, that's what I did. We even talked about getting married, and I thought we were going in that direction. I went over today to spend time with him and clean up. This sorry piece of crap told me that he doesn't feel that things are going in the right direction, and we needed to take a break.

Led by Anxiety

It has been about a month that I've been dating this guy. Oh, I like him! He's been consistent with calls, texts, and Zoom almost daily. We have spent lots of time getting to know each other. Today he told me that he would be busy doing some yard work and he would call me later. Well, it's been about 5 hours, and he hasn't called me yet. My anxiety drives me crazy; I want to text and call him all the time.

What is Wrong with Me?

My boyfriend of almost a year is a narcissist! He is the opposite of me, and I still don't have the guts to leave him. I am freaking out because I love him, and I don't know what life would be like without him. What is wrong with me? I know I need to leave, and he is not suitable for me, but I am so afraid to start over. I am tired of starting over with boyfriend after boyfriend.

Sign Them Papers (Usher song)

My boyfriend of a year wants to move in with me. The problem is, I own my own home and don't want to risk any issues with it. So, I asked him to sign a cohabitation contract, and he declined. My boyfriend said it makes no sense to sign a cohabitation contract because we love each other and plan to get married. I love and don't want to lose him. Do you think I should just forget about the cohabitation contract not to lose him?

His Realization

How does a man begin to date you and then say he's not ready to be in a relationship? After almost four months of Zoom dating, I thought everything was going great. But last week, he ended things because he said he realized he should not be dating because he is not ready.

Ms. Clingy

I have been dating this guy for about a month. I like him and do think he is the one. But then I noticed for the last week he's not been as interested as before. He doesn't call or text as he used to, and when I call or text, he doesn't respond. Finally, I asked him what was going on and that I thought we had hit it off nicely.

My boyfriend said he didn't mean to be mean but that I was too clingy. I'm struggling with his comment because I've been super-mindful about my behavior. I've tried not being too clingy, but I did let him know that I am interested in him. I thought I was communicating my interest healthily. I don't understand why men seem interested, but then they run away from me.

Self-Esteem Blow

I met and went out with three guys in 2019, all of whom I just knew was my husband. But for some reason, they all ran for the hills. These rejections are a massive blow to my self-esteem; I keep wondering why they don't stick around. Men running away from me do not help me achieve my goal of having a husband and kids. I am almost 40 years old—when will I find a boyfriend that wants to be with me? I cannot help but think that maybe I'm doing something wrong.

Always Available

I invested almost six months into a man. I spent countless hours on the phone trying to get to know him, only for him to ghost me. I think grown men ghosting women is so childish. What's wrong with merely explaining to me that he's no longer interested? He says he wanted a woman who shows interest in him. I showed him interest! And I told him several times that I was interested in him and wanted something more. I was always available to talk and text. Maybe he doesn't know what he wants?

She Ain't Even Pretty

I was dating this guy for almost a year, only to find out on Instagram that he got engaged. How is that possible when I was at his house nearly every week? I am shocked and offended! The girl he proposed to ain't even pretty. When I tried to let her know that he was cheating on us, they both blocked me.

Frequent Flyer Miles

Whatever happened to maturity and common decency? Five months of talking, texting, and zooming, and now he seems to have fallen off the face of the earth? Twice I flew to visit him because he said he did not have the money to visit me. Then, one morning I woke up after my last visit to see that he blocked me on all social media platforms. I wish he would have told me what I did wrong; I have no closure to move on. I felt he was my husband. And I was even ready to move to his home state to be with him. I don't know what I did wrong.

Opposite Directions

My boyfriend and I have been together for eight months. Last week out of the blue, he said he thinks we're going in the opposite direction. When I asked him why he thought so, he said we just were. After eight months together, I feel as if he owes me an explanation of why he thinks we are going in opposite directions. Eight months is a long time to waste someone's time. I thought we were going to get married. We talked about our future together and made plans, only now for him to say that we are going in opposite directions? What the heck does that even mean?

But He Introduced Me to His Family

My boyfriend and I have been together for almost a year now. Things have been going great between us, so I let him move in with me after three weeks of knowing each other. And from day one, I told him that we're going to get married. I was so excited when he took me to his family's 4th of July cookout. All his family loved me, and his parents were all smiles.

But a week later, he broke things off with me with no explanation. It makes no sense that he introduced me to his family only to break up with me a week later. Why did he waste my time for almost a year if he was just gonna dump me with no explanation given? Why are men so immature and heartless?

Grown Men Don't Do That

For three months, my boyfriend and I were like white on rice. We spent almost every day together. And he practically moved into my spot since he was here so much. For once, I thought things were looking up for me because I finally met someone with whom I thought we clicked. Lately, I noticed he wasn't coming over as much. He has been ignoring my calls and messages. When I messaged him on social media, he didn't respond. And when I text him, he would read them but not reply. Shortly after his communication slowed down, he blocked me with no explanation. How do you call yourself a mature man yet not communicate that you don't want to date me anymore? A whole grown 30-year-old man does not just stop talking to you and go silent when they are no longer interested.

DNA Test

I shacked up with my boyfriend for a year. Six months into us living together, I found out I was pregnant. I told him to marry me, and he said he wasn't ready to get married. So, he moved out and said he's gonna need a DNA test once the baby comes. What the heck? Does he think I am a whore or something? We lived together for six months and were having unprotected sex. Now he wants a DNA test.

5 Years a Girlfriend

Two Whole Babies Later

I am so fed up with my baby daddy of four years. I told him when we got together that I wanted to get married. He still has not asked me to marry him. I don't know what to do to get him to marry me. I cannot stand the thought of starting over. We have a whole baby and another one on the way. When I left my other baby daddy of five years, I promised that the next man would marry me. Two babies later, and still nothing.

Boyfriend Renters' Rights

My boyfriend and I have been living together for almost four years. It was my house, and I allowed him to move in. We agreed to split the bills. But he said I had to pay more because I have two kids, and it was just him. A month ago, we had a massive fight about money and him staying out late.

So, we broke up, and I asked him to move out. Could you believe this low-down piece of crap, sorry excuse for a man, took me to court because he said he had renters' rights? This fool wants me to sell my house and split the profits with him! Is he for real? I'm gonna have to get a lawyer to get me out of this mess!

New Neighbor

My ex-boyfriend of five years moved out of my house just to move right down the street with the neighbor he cheated on me with.

Then six months later, he proposed to her. Unbelievable! This man told me that he didn't want to get married. So, how is he now ready to get married to a chick he's known for six months?

Dating for Marriage

I met my boyfriend when I was a sophomore in college. I told him that I want us to at least get engaged by the time I graduated. And shortly after the engagement, we should get married, I told him. After graduation, he took me to a nice restaurant, and I thought he would propose. After all, I had met all his family and friends.

To my surprise, he told me that he had gotten married to the woman he was dating while he was dating me. How in the world did this man get married without me knowing? I am still in disbelief! I am so embarrassed and ashamed. I have him plastered all over my social media and told everyone we were gonna get married.

Got Married

My boyfriend of five years recently dumped me. When I asked him how he could throw away five years, he said he had some things he needed to work out with his family. In less than a week, this "...cursed word...." proposed to some chick on Instagram. Five whole years, this fool wasted my time with promises of getting married, only for him to marry someone he met six months ago.

Not Interested Anymore

I have been shacking up with my boyfriend for almost four years. I asked him when he was gonna propose to me because we discussed getting married. He said he was also saving up for a ring and wedding. After four years, he broke up with me because he was no longer interested or attracted to me anymore. Then he moved his things out and got his apartment. So, I've been stalking his social media, and he got some new girl up there calling her wifey.

Marriage Pressure

My boyfriend and I dated for five years. We have a little girl. When I asked him when was he going to marry me, he said I was pressuring him. That pissed me the heck off. How I'm I pressuring him to marry me after five years? Then to make things worse, I found sexual texts and pictures on his phone. So, I kicked that filthy piece of crap out of my apartment. It's not like he was helping me with bills anyway.

Would you believe that bastard married some chick in a year? They have two more kids living in a decent house to date. And my baby and I are living in the hood. Five years I wasted with this man, and he didn't even propose it to me. Thankfully, their marriage didn't work out and only lasted seven years, but it still bugs me after all these years. Karma is a wretch! I wasted all those years having sex, washing, cooking, having his baby, and working two jobs to help us make ends meet, only for him to marry some other woman. SMH!

50 Years of Marriage

Marriage is significant because my grandparents were married for almost 50 years. I have always dreamed of having a marriage like them. They have been the perfect example for me. But, marriage is not essential to my boyfriend of nearly five years. I keep asking him when will he marry me, and he continues to give me excuses. Then we had a huge fight about us not being married, and he yelled out that he would never marry me. I don't even know what to do now. I just knew in my heart of hearts that we were gonna get married. My boyfriend has shattered my dreams of getting married.

Government Sanctioned Paper

My boyfriend and I have been together for five years. I want to get married, but he doesn't. I do love him and don't want to rock the boat. I know deep down that he loves me, but he doesn't want to get married. I told him that I have always wanted to get married and have the house with the white picket fence, 2.5 kids, and a dog. He said we could have all of that without the piece of government paper. But I want that piece of paper!

His, Mine, and Ours

I have been taking care of my boyfriend's two kids and mine that I had before. Plus, we have one child together. I have been caring for all the children for five years. I asked him when is he gonna marry me since I am investing so much in taking care of him and his kids. He said right now he's not ready to get married. When I asked him when would he be ready to get married, and he said when the kids are older. Did I mention that his kids are six and seven years old? And our son is four years old. How much older does he want the kids to get before he marries me? I don't understand it at all! I feel like he's just using me to raise his kids.

All my Boyfriends

Recently, I asked my boyfriend of almost five years why he hasn't asked me to marry him yet. He said he wasn't ready to get married. I burst out in tears, sobbing uncontrollably. I feel like there is something wrong with me because he hasn't asked me to marry him. This has happened to me so often. I feel unlovable at 35 years old. I gave so much to my boyfriends, yet not one has asked me to marry them. What is wrong with me?

Shack up Test

My boyfriend and I have been dating for almost four years. I asked him when he would marry me, and he said we should live together before we get married. I don't want to live with any man until I get married anymore. In the past, I have lived with other boyfriends, and none of them married me. I have three other kids, and we have one together. I love him and don't want to lose him. What should I do?

Another Five Years?

My boyfriend and I have been together for five years now. I helped him to move from his last girl's house to mine. He swore he's gonna marry me, but how long does it take? I asked him when is he gonna marry me, and he said he's not ready now but will be soon. But he didn't have an exact timetable. I don't see myself waiting another five years for him to marry me.

No More Kids out of Wedlock

My boyfriend and I have been together for almost five years. And we have three children together. My mom gave me some money from a lawsuit and told me to buy a home. I mentioned this to my boyfriend about the money and house, and he asked what about him? So, I asked him when was he gonna marry me, and he said he had not thought about it. I told my boyfriend that I wanted to get married from day one. Also, I told him that I want us to have two more kids. I also told him that I don't want to have any more kids out of wedlock. Why can't he just go ahead and marry me?

Waiting for Him to be Ready

I've been crying for six months straight because I broke up with my boyfriend of five years. I wanted marriage, and he said he's not sure if that's what he wants. I told him that I would wait for him to be ready. But he said he didn't see himself getting ready any time soon. Deep down, I knew that meant that he didn't want to marry me. But I love him so much! I know I need to move on, but why is it so hard to let go?

Fat, Ugly, and Desperate

I'm still trying to figure out how my boyfriend of four years was married, and I didn't know! He traveled for work and could only be in town on weekends and a few days here and there. Now, I realize that he works in my state on the weekends and goes home to his wife and three kids for the week. His wife called and cussed me out, calling me a homewrecker and told me how I destroyed their family. This fool told his wife that he was dating me because I was fat, ugly, no one wanted me, and I was desperate.

Gone with the Ring

My boyfriend of four years broke up with me while I was sleeping. Early one morning, I woke up, and he was gone. I called to find out why he left, and he said he hated being pressured into getting married. So, I asked him what about the ring I found hidden in his drawer. He said it was fake, and he's gonna take it back to the store to get his money back. I couldn't believe that my boyfriend I loved so much, and my ring was gone.

Just Another Woman

My boyfriend and I have been dating for almost five years. We live together and have one baby. And he has another child from a previous relationship. Well, the baby momma looked me in my face and told me that I was just another woman my boyfriend is using, and he won't marry me. When I told my boyfriend this, he said not to pay any attention to his baby momma. And that his baby momma is just a bitter black woman. So, I asked him when are we gonna get married, and he said he wasn't ready yet. Now, I cannot help but think that his baby momma might be right!

Marriage is my Goal

I broke up with my boyfriend after four years of dating. When I agreed to shack up with him, I told him that marriage was my goal. Year after year, he would promise marriage. But after four years, still nothing. Every time I asked him when was he gonna marry me, he would say a part of him is not ready. How many years does it take for a man to be ready? And what does he mean by a part of him is not ready?

Please Marry Me

I just celebrated five years with my boyfriend, and I am so depressed! We have a child together, and I'm about to be thirty years old. I want another baby and for him to marry me. For the last five years, I have been trying to make the family thing work for us, but it has not happened. I have begged and pleaded for my baby daddy to commit to our baby and me and ask me to marry him. My momma said I need to move on. But my baby daddy and I currently live together and split bills 50/50. So, I cannot afford my own place. Plus, I don't want to start over and bring a new man around my baby. I don't know what to do to make him marry me.

Too Young

I have been with my boyfriend since I was 15. I always wanted to get married before having children. But I got pregnant at sixteen. We just celebrated our tenth anniversary. I asked my baby daddy when was he gonna marry me? He said we are too young to get married. I told him that I think twenty-five is a perfect age for us to get married. But I guess twenty-five is kind of young to be getting married.

10 Years a Girlfriend

How Long Does It Take?

Ten years, four kids, and a house later, my baby daddy still hasn't married me yet. When I ask him when he's gonna marry me, he said he hasn't decided if he wanted to get married yet. How long does it take for a man to decide if he wants to marry me or not? It has been ten years already! Surely, that's more than enough time for him to marry me.

How Many More Excuses?

After ten years, I thought my boyfriend had run out of excuses for why he has not married me or at least proposed. This time, the excuse was he doesn't like how I treat his teenage daughter. That is such bullcrap. I have known that little girl since she was three, and I treat her just like mine. I am so tired of the excuses for him not marrying me. I don't know how much more I can take. But I have already invested ten years in this relationship. The thought of starting over makes me scared.

Still Hoping?

After eight years of living together, I have finally accepted that my boyfriend will never marry me. I am so torn, because I love him so much. And I want to spend the rest of my life with him. But how long will it take for him to marry me? Even though I feel that he will never marry me, I am still hoping that he will ask me one day. After all this time, I just don't want to have to start over.

He Cannot Marry Me Because?

I just found out that I was pregnant. So, I told my boyfriend of almost ten years that he needs to marry me because I don't want to have any babies out of wedlock. To my surprise, my boyfriend tells me that he can't marry me because he's already married. He said he's married to his childhood sweetheart, who doesn't have her legal status to stay in the United States. So, to keep his childhood sweetheart from being deported, he married her. Are you kidding me? Ten years, I wasted my life waiting for this man to marry me, and he's already married?

They Think I Am Already His Wife

I am getting tired of being a girlfriend to my live-in boyfriend of almost nine years. He doesn't have any kids, but I already have one when we got together. I want to have more children, but he said he is not ready to have kids yet. My son loves him, so I don't want to break up our happy home. I do so much as his girl that many think I'm already his wife.

Lately, I find myself asking him what's the holdup on him marrying me. Sadly he will not give me an honest answer. He says I need to be patient and wait until he's ready to marry me. But after ten years, how much more time does he need? How much longer do I need to be patient for him to marry me?

Marry Me Before our Fourth Kid

Ten years, three kids, another one on the way, and my boyfriend still has not married me yet. I want to be at least engaged by the time our baby comes. I don't want to have another baby in sin. I've been thinking of telling him that I want him to marry me now. But I don't want to come off as telling him what to do. In the past, he has said that my nagging and pushing is not going to make him want to marry me any sooner. I don't know how else to communicate to him that he needs to marry me now?

Microscope Needed

I begged my boyfriend of seven years to propose, or else I would pack up the kids and leave. So, he gave in and proposed. The ring is so tiny that I cried. You almost need a microscope to see it. I cannot believe this. And it's not like he doesn't have the money. Is this all I am worth to him?

My House and Ring

I helped my boyfriend of nine years to move out of his mother's house and in with me. I helped him to find a good job and fix his credit. We planned to get married once our money got right. We also planned to buy a house in a nice community. Only for that (curse word) to save up, buy a home, and got married. That (curse word) put that skankish wife in what should have been MY HOUSE!!

That witch got my ring and my house! After I invested all that time, energy, and effort to get (curse word) to the place he needs to be? So that he could be the husband I need him to be. Only for him to leave me for another woman. Yes, I am mad and bitter about that Sugar Honey Iced Tea!

Tired of Struggling

I met my college sweetheart in my freshman year. We've been together for ten years. Over the years, I have begged him to marry me. Last Christmas, he finally proposed, but truthfully, I am so tired of struggling with him. After ten years of struggling, I am exhausted! At almost 30 years old, I'm tired of struggling with my boyfriend and all the hurt and pain he has put me through. I'm tired of trying to build him so he can be right. I would love to meet a man that's already made and has his stuff together. I don't want a man that I must hold his hands and lead him. I feel like I have three sons instead of two.

I Found My Engagement Ring

My baby daddy and I have been together for almost ten years. I've been asking him, year after year, when was he gonna marry me. But he always said he wasn't ready to get married yet. Last month I found my engagement ring in his closet. So that means he's about to propose to me, right? It's a lovely ring, and I cannot wait for him to propose to me.

But I am shocked that he spent that much money on it. I know we didn't have that much money in our joint savings. So where did he get all that money? It's really bothering me. Plus, I had told him that I didn't want him to spend too much money buying an engagement ring.

Also, I told him that I would take anything at this point because I was so tired of waiting for him to propose. Well, Valentine's day came, and I got all dressed up and waited at home for him. I just knew we would go out and have a good time and get engaged. But he called and said he had to work late. I was disappointed because I was excited for him to propose. He never came home. Then I found out on Facebook that my future husband had proposed to some other chick with MY RING!!

Will You Marry Me?

I've been with my boyfriend for nine years. I got tired of asking him when he would marry me and make an honest woman out of me. We have three kids together. It's not like he's going anywhere, so why hasn't he proposed? So, I proposed to him with a nice ring, and he said no—he told me he is not ready to get married. I am so embarrassed by this whole mess. How could he say no to marrying me?

Spender Vs. Saver

After ten years and four babies with my baby daddy, this lousy piece of crap tells me that he's not gonna marry me because I waste too much of his money. What the heck I'm I supposed to do? He makes $110K per year, and he is complaining about me spending too much money? That's fine! We will see how he feels when I put his behind on child support!

Marry My Best Friend

My boyfriend and I have been best friends since my high school sophomore year. He promised to give me forever, every time I asked him when was he gonna marry me. So, I have been expecting an engagement ring because we have always talked about getting married. And even though he said he wasn't ready to get married, I just thought maybe he had cold feet.

Shockingly, after eight years of waiting for him to marry me, he dumped me on Christmas. He even deleted me from all his social media platforms. I'm feeling so much anger and resentment because I believed in making a man your best friend and then marrying him. But my best friend doesn't want to marry me. I thought spending time becoming a man's best friend would guarantee him marrying me.

God Forgot to Tell Him

I am in my early 50s. I have always wanted to get married and prayed for God to send me my husband my whole life. And I believe the Lord has sent him to me. But he says God has not spoken to him about marrying me. We've been on and off for over eight years. And now I'm wondering how much longer will it be for God to speak to him? From the first time I met him, I knew he was supposed to be my husband.

The Lord told me that he was my husband. But now, I feel as if my life has passed me by. I don't want to let him go. I know we're supposed to get married because God told me that he was my husband. So, I'm just going to continue to trust the Lord to speak to him.

He Said He Wanted to Get Married Too

I dated my ex-boyfriend for almost ten years. When we got together, I told him that I wanted to get married. He said he wanted to get married too. Great, we're both on the same page, I thought. But first, he wanted to buy a home. So, I let him move in with me to save money. Recently, I found out he was looking at houses, and I got so excited. I asked him how come he didn't tell me so that I can pick the house out. He said he wanted it to be a surprise. Shortly after that, he told me that he was moving out. I asked him why he wanted to move out if we're trying to save money for a house. A few months later, he broke down and told me that he bought a house, but it wasn't for him and me.

My boyfriend said he had met someone else who he knew was the one for him. So, he proposed to her. I think I might have blacked out or something. I couldn't believe that he would treat me like that. It broke my heart that I invested so much into him only for him to propose to another woman and buy her a house? But what about me and all the plans we made together?

Marry the Virgin

I've been with my boyfriend for ten years. I was still a virgin when I got with him in my early 20s. I told him that I wanted to get married, and he said he did too. But I felt like he was holding marriage over my head because we argued all the time about us getting married. Finally, he broke up with me and married somebody else after a few months. I feel like such a fool for wasting all this time with him. And now I'm in my thirties, I feel like a fish out of water. I feel so depressed and used by him. I'm not sure where to go from here.

Shaping Him for Who?

I'm torn about sticking it through with my boyfriend of nine years. He doesn't make a lot of money, but I love him. However, I can't do the struggle love and life with him. I am frustrated because I'm putting so much energy into shaping this man who might not even marry me. After nine years, he has not even brought up marrying me, not one time. I feel like I'm stuck between a rock and a hard place. I cannot help but think that I'm shaping him for another woman to have.

Resentment

I have been with my younger boyfriend for almost ten years. He was twenty-five, and I was thirty-five when we started dating. When I met him, he had nothing and was living from pillar to post. But he was so charming, and the sex was out of this world. So, I allowed him to move in with me to my house. Back then, he made promises of us getting married but first, he needed to get on his feet.

Ten years later, I am still waiting for him to marry me. He hasn't brought up marriage in years. So, I asked him when was he gonna marry me.

My boyfriend is still claiming that he's trying to get himself together. Now I realize that I resent him for all the help I have given him, and he still hasn't asked me to marry him. After ten years, I am not sure if he was using me to help him get on his feet or if he loves me for real.

I Didn't Know

After dating my boyfriend on and off for ten years, I found out that he was married on Facebook. When I confronted him, he claimed he was separated, so technically, he wasn't married. It still bugs me that I didn't know he was married because I don't believe in messing with another woman's man. We even lived together for a short time, and I had no clue he was married. But he moved out because he said living together without being married was a sin. So, I asked him when he was gonna marry me, and he started acting funny towards me. I was ok with him moving out because I was busy finishing up my master's degree.

And I was working two jobs to pay for it. It kills me that I keep running back to him even after discovering that he was married. And all that time, I was begging him to marry me. I guess it all makes sense now. He's still broke, but he always delivered in the bedroom. Yes, I am a victim of the ghetto dingaling.

He has Cold Feet

My boyfriend of eight years dumped me because he didn't want to get married. I don't understand why he wasted eight years of my life to finally come out and tell me that he didn't want to get married. Okay, sure, he has said a few times that he didn't think marriage was for him, but I just thought he had cold feet.

Irish Twins and No Marriage

My boyfriend and I got pregnant three months into our relationship. So, I allowed him to move in with me. But deep down on the inside, I knew I shouldn't have let him move in with me because he was not working. A month after our first son was born, I got pregnant again. I had two kids, one-year-old Irish twins. The boys are now 5 and 6, and still no marriage. I am getting impatient, so I went and bought a ring so he could propose to me. Can you believe he told me that he's not ready to get married yet?

Pissed

My relationship with my baby daddy was already in troubled waters, and this pandemic is not helping. Now that we are stuck at home 24/7, I am pissed that he hasn't married me yet—nine years, and still nothing. I want to break up with him after COVID-19, but I feel guilty because he doesn't have a job.

Summer Fling

I started dating my boyfriend when I was 34. He was ten years younger. It began as a summer fling with lots of sex. Well, that summer fling ended up with us shacking up for almost ten years. Over the years, I pressed him about marrying me, and he said that he was just having fun and wasn't ready to get married. So, I'm now in my mid-40s, trying to start over to try and get married. Ten whole years wasted with this child!

His Last Name

I've been with my boyfriend going on eight years. On our eighth anniversary, I asked him when he was gonna give me his last name.

To my surprise, my boyfriend said he doesn't want to get married. How is this possible when I have always made it plain that I wanted to get married?

The New Baby Momma

After almost nine years with my boyfriend and my son's father, I can't help but wonder why he didn't ask me to marry him. When I asked him why he hasn't asked me to marry him, he kept saying he doesn't want to get married. But I have always made it clear that I wanted to get married. I told him that we had a family. What does my boyfriend mean he doesn't want to get married? So, I gave him an ultimatum to propose, or we would be over. Instead of proposing, he moved out and moved in with another woman. She is now six months pregnant.

And guess what? He proposed to her. I don't understand why didn't he ask to marry him after all this time. It just doesn't make any sense that he waited and made me wait only for him not to choose to propose to me but propose to his new baby mamma instead. I need closure from him because this makes no sense.

Santa Didn't Come

I've been with my boyfriend for seven years. I am trying to figure out if I need to wait for him to marry me or move on. How long does it take for a man to decide if he wants to marry me or not? After seven years of being his girlfriend, he didn't even give me a Christmas present or stopped by for dinner. It hurts!

Girlfriend

I've been with my kids' father for seven years now. He has yet to say that I am his girlfriend. Neither has he committed to marrying me. We have kids together; he should marry me and keep our family together. When I ask him when we will get married, he says he's not ready to make such a commitment. The crazy thing is, I am so in love with him—he was my first everything. Sometimes, I wonder if he loves his other baby mamas more than me. Why can't he realize how much I love him and want to marry him?

Family Dream

Ten years! That's how long it has taken me to realize that the dream of having a family with my childhood love and kids' father will never happen.

Deep down, I want to walk away, but I feel stuck with him. I just don't want any other woman around my kids if he dates someone else.

Three Abortions for a Marriage

I've been with my boyfriend for nine years. And I have had three abortions because he said he didn't want to have any kids out of wedlock. So, I went ahead and aborted the babies because I loved him and wanted to be the perfect wife. After abortion number three, I was hoping for a proposal. He's been promising me that he's gonna marry me. Instead, my boyfriend broke up with me and proposed to one of those "church girls" that held out sex for marriage. I feel so stupid for wasting all my youthful days with that fool. And now I have nothing to show for all those wasted years.

I Want Him to Be the One

My boyfriend and I have been together for eight years. And we have three beautiful children. My parents were divorced, which caused our family to split up. Therefore, stability is critical for me. To date, my boyfriend still has not asked me to marry him. I want my kids to have the life I didn't have with both parents. Even though I want him to marry, honestly, I don't think he is the one for me. But I want him to be the one. How do I leave with three kids and no job in my early 30s?

I Built Him

I've been building a relationship with my boyfriend for eight years. When I got pregnant last year, I asked him about getting married. My boyfriend said marriage was the last thing on his mind and that he just wanted to stash some cash right now. I was speechless. I asked him when will he get marriage on his mind, and he said he don't know. I mean, after investing and building him up for eight years, I'm wondering if this is worth fighting for? Where am I going to go with a newborn baby?

While Living with Me

I've been with my daughter's father on and off for almost ten years. All those years, I've asked and begged him to marry me. He always said he wasn't ready to get married. So, if he wasn't ready to get married, please tell me how he married another woman while we were still together? I thought I was having a nightmare when he told me.

I couldn't believe he would do me like that. My baby daddy confessed it all to me after he and his wife fell out, and she put him out. Disappointedly, I took him back. That's how I got pregnant again. I was such a fool to believe he wanted to make things work with me. Three months later, he went back with his wife!

No End of How Long I Will Wait

I don't care what people say. I love my boyfriend! And when you love someone, there's no end to how long you'll wait for him to ask you to marry him. I love him, and I will wait for him to marry me. I've been waiting for my boyfriend to ask me to marry him for ten years now. But there is no limit if you love each other. And my boyfriend and I love each other. I wouldn't be with him if we didn't love each other. We have a beautiful relationship, and we are sticking together. Okay, sure, he got some chick pregnant, but I love my boyfriend to no end. And if I must wait forever, then so be it. When he is ready to marry me, he will.

Still Searching

It's been almost ten years since my boyfriend, and I have been living together with our three children. I want to get married, but he says he's not ready yet. However, he cannot say when he will be ready to marry me. My girlfriend recently told me that she saw my boyfriend's picture on a dating site. I asked him about it, and he denied it. So, I cussed her out and told her that she was jealous of me. But my intuition kept messing with me about my friend saying she saw my man on a dating site.

So, one night, I started to do some digging. And would you believe I found my boyfriend on not only one dating site but a few others? It devastated me because I thought we were happy. Even though he said he wasn't ready to get married, we talked about getting engaged by Christmas. So why is he out here shopping around for other women on dating sites?

He Doesn't Want to Have Kids

I dated my boyfriend for ten years. He said he didn't want to have kids, so I said, why the heck not? He said he didn't want to have kids yet. So, I decided that I would wait for him to be ready to have children because he was a good guy. Gurl, why this 'curse word' left me and married some chick he met in less than a year? The worst part is, they have three kids now! I would never do that again. I wasted ten years of my life waiting for a fool to be ready to have children with me. I also thought we were going to get married. I feel like a fool. That mess still pisses me off all these years later.

I Ain't Seen Nothing Wrong with a Lil Shacking Up

My boyfriend and I have successfully been living together for ten years. My mother, aunts, and cousins did the same. And some of them are now married. Those are perfect examples for me to follow. So, I don't see nothing wrong with a lil shacking up before getting married.

Sure, some women like me are still waiting to be married. But lots of couples did it, and it worked out well for them! I trust my boyfriend that he will marry me when he's ready. Times have changed, and there are no set rules about living together before marriage. I think it's an intelligent thing to do before committing to someone for the rest of your life.

Five Month Proposal

I was with my baby daddy for nine years. Before me, he was with his other baby mama for four years. Shockingly he broke up with me and proposed to a chick after five months. I cannot believe that he married that girl in one year after I wasted nine years with that fool.

On and Off for Ten Years

My boyfriend and I have been together for ten years on and off. I've never been married but have always wanted to be. But he still hasn't asked me to marry him. I've questioned my boyfriend and my relationship a few times because he never wants to talk about getting married. I feel like I should leave, but I want us to work so badly!

Proposal After He Got Her Pregnant

My live-in-boyfriend and I have been together for nine years. I have begged my boyfriend over the years for us to get married. But he always said he wasn't ready to get married. Then I found out that he got some chick pregnant. So now, suddenly, my boyfriend wants to propose to me? After I've been begging him for years to marry me? So, is he proposing because he loves me? I don't know what pisses me off more—that he cheated or that he didn't think enough of me to wrap it up. Now, after almost ten years of begging him to marry me, he wants to propose. I am so torn on what to do.

Friends with Benefits

My boyfriend and I dated for five years. I wanted to get married, but he didn't. So, he broke up with me. But even though we've broken up, we've been friends with benefits for the last four years. But then I stopped. I was having a weak moment, so I called him for a nightcap. He came over, and one thing led to the other, and what do you know? We made passionate love, and I got knocked up! So, I asked him if, since I'm pregnant, this is more of a reason to get married. He said he is not ready to get married yet. I just cannot see myself being a single mom—so embarrassing in my culture!

Baecation Turned Wifey

My ex-boyfriend and I were together for ten years. I have always wanted to get married, and I told him that from the beginning. But, whenever I brought up marriage, he would say he was not ready to get married. I often reminded him that I told him I wanted to get married. Well, this boyfriend of mine who told me for ten years that he wasn't ready to get married went on a trip, found a new girlfriend, and never came back home.

I cried and stayed in a fetal position for days! I heard through the grapevine that he is now engaged to her. I cannot explain the resentment I have for that man! And to make matters worse, he came to our apartment while I was at work and took all of his stuff. That was such a cowardly move.

He Loves Me, and He Loves Me Not

Almost ten years of washing, cooking, cleaning, sexing, and birthing his babies, for my boyfriend to tell me that he doesn't love me the way I love him. So, all this time he's been saying he loves me is a lie? The truth is, I do love him so much. And after all these years, it hurts like heck when my boyfriend said he doesn't love me the way I love him. I just thought if I played the wifey role, he would finally see me as wife material. I love him so much, and I cannot imagine my life without him.

I Want More Kids

My baby daddy and I have been together for nine years. Lately, I noticed he has been distant. When I asked him why he seems so distant, he denied that he was. After weeks of trying to get to the bottom of why he's been so distant, I finally got him to tell me the truth. My boyfriend says he doesn't want any more kids. My boyfriend not wanting to have any more kids is a crazy mess. I have always wanted to have a big family. So why doesn't he want to have any more children? Then I asked him when we would get married, and he said he doesn't want to get married.

My heart dropped because I've never been married, and I just want one man to call my husband. I want a pretty, big ring that says I'm taken. I asked him if he thinks he could change his mind, and he said it was possible. I've already invested nine years with him and three kids. So, I think I might as well try and stick it through. I love him so much, and I want to be with him forever. And if it takes forever, I want him to be my husband. I don't even know how I'm gonna tell him that I'm pregnant again. What if that drives him away?

A Hoe?

I slept with my boyfriend of six years on the first night. About three months ago, I overheard him telling his brother that he's not going to marry me cause I'm a hoe. I almost cussed his trifling tail out, but I kept my cool. A hoe? It takes two to tango, but he's calling me a hoe. The mother of his children he calls a hoe and doesn't want to marry me! These men are the worst!

Diapers and Formula

My boyfriend and I have been together for ten years. I just had our second child, and I'm on maternity leave with no pay. He wants me to pay half his credit card bill when I return to work. Can you believe this crap? I helped this man to work on and build his credit. When he was homeless and didn't have a pot to piss in or a window to throw it through, I let him move in with me. And now he wants me to pay half his bill because I ask him for money to buy diapers and formula for our baby. This fool done lost his mind!! He's crazy if he thinks I'm gonna pay a penny on his credit card.

A Woman's Intuition

I've been dating my boyfriend for almost ten years. And I told him from day one that I wanted to get married. Over the years, I've asked him when he was gonna marry me, and he said soon. Although he keeps saying he's gonna marry me, for some reason, my intuition tells me that he isn't. I don't know what to think. Do I believe my boyfriend, who's the love of my life? Or do I believe my intuition?

My Fate?

My boyfriend and I have been together since college. I have always wanted to get married. Now I'm wondering if he'll ever marry me. After ten years, does it make sense to get up and leave just because my boyfriend has not married me yet? It is so hard to start over. I hear so many women talk about how they wasted their lives with someone just for him to leave and marry someone else within a year. I pray to God; this is not my fate.

Why Spoil A Good Thing?

I am 30 years old and have been with my boyfriend for ten years. He proposed to me seven years ago when we found out I was pregnant. Three years later, when I asked him when he would marry me, he asked, why spoil a good thing? At this point, I think I'm just done with men. I wasted all these years, and still nothing. I feel like such a fool for wasting all this time waiting for him to marry me.

Not Good Enough

My boyfriend and I have been together for ten years. I keep asking him when he will marry me, and he said if it's not broken, then why try to fix it? I was stunned, and I burst out crying. I'm good enough to shack up with and take care of him and his kids plus mine, but I'm not good enough to marry? After ten years of hoping and praying that my boyfriend would marry me, what do I do now?

Weddings are Expensive

My boyfriend and I have been together for almost ten years. After baby number two, he proposed. But we still haven't gotten married yet. When I asked him when he would marry me, he said that weddings are too expensive. I asked him about going to the courthouse, and he said for me to just wait for a while. But It's been five years since he proposed. So how much longer I'm I supposed to wait? Sometimes, I feel like he's just stringing me along.

He Wants to Get Married Too

I was 35 when I started dating my boyfriend. I told him that I wanted to get married, and he said he wanted to get married too. Cool, we both wanted to get married, so we're on the same track. Well, it's been ten years, and he still hasn't asked me to marry him yet. And now

I'm looking back at how I wasted years with this man. After all these years, we're still splitting bills. When will he marry me and take over our family's financial responsibility? I don't even know what to do. At this age, I feel so tired and don't feel like starting all over again.

Why Can't He Just Marry Me?

My boyfriend and I have been together for eight years. He has always said he doesn't want to get married. After our second child, I asked him if he changed his mind about getting married. Unfortunately, he said he still doesn't want to get married. I don't understand it. We have a wonderful life and beautiful kids. Why can't he just marry me?

Go Home to Yo Baby Mama

I am a firm believer that when a man meets you, in no time, he will know if he will marry you or not. My now husband was shacking up with his kids' mom for twelve years. He met me and expressed interest in me, and I told him to go home to his baby mama. He moved out in two weeks, proposed to me in six months, and a year later, we got married. And we just celebrated our 20th anniversary.

Peace Made

I've had many long-term boyfriends, but none of them wanted to marry me. Now, at forty-five years old, I think of all the years I wasted waiting for my boyfriends to marry me. My last relationship lasted seven years, and I had a baby for him. I think I have made peace with never getting married. I don't understand why none of my boyfriends wanted to marry me.

Long Term Investment

Ten years of shacking up with my boyfriend and two kids later, only for him to tell me that he's not sure if he wants to marry me. He said he doesn't see me as a long-term investment. My boyfriend has only worked part-time since I have known him, but he makes good money. It's funny how he wants to talk about how I am not a long-term investment, but he wouldn't even know what investment means if it weren't for me. The nerve of him!

More Than Enough Time

I was with my baby daddy for ten years. He was a social worker and was our breadwinner. I broke it off with him because I thought ten years was more than enough time for him to marry me. But in no time after we broke up, this sorry behind man married some girl he met in six months.

Commitment Ring

My boyfriend and I have been together for ten years. He gave me a ring, but it's more of a commitment ring than an engagement ring. Sadly, I don't think we will ever get married. We have three kids, a lovely house, and we live like we are married, so he said he doesn't see the point in us getting married.

Broadway Dancer

My boyfriend and I dated throughout college. I would always talk to him about us getting married. And he would always say he doesn't see marriage in his future. I figured that he was scared, so I stuck it through in hopes that his mind would change. Two years out of college, he broke up with me because he said he didn't want the same things I did.

Furthermore, he said it wasn't right for me to keep sticking around waiting for him to marry me. Less than six months later, he got engaged to a Broadway dancer and married a year after that! The problem is, I need closure. How come, after all those years, my boyfriend wouldn't marry me but turned around and married a girl he barely knew?

Breaking News

Just found out that my boyfriend of almost eight years doesn't want to get married. I am so lost for words. I want to be a wife and not a girlfriend; I deserve a man who will make a total commitment to me. I love him so much, and I want him to marry me, but he doesn't want to get married.

He Proposed So

My boyfriend proposed after six months of us being together. So, I allowed him to move in with me to save money. However, now, I have an issue with this arrangement because I have been the only one who has kept a job these last ten years. We can't even do 50/50 because he can only afford to pay the cable bill for most months. I am starting to think that he is with me because I can provide.

God Told Him I Was His Wife

My boyfriend and I met in church. We became remarkably close. He told me that God told him that I was his wife. So, in secret, we moved in together, and in less than a year, I was pregnant. I felt so ashamed that I stopped going to church. We were boyfriend and girlfriend for ten years, and the babies kept coming. Every year he would promise me marriage. Yet, last year, he married another sister in our same church without me knowing.

Dream Woman

After almost ten years, I realized that my boyfriend sold me a dream. Why? In one of our arguments about why he hasn't married me, he said I am not his dream woman or the one he wants. My boyfriend said he would marry the one he wants to marry and make a family. Ten years, this man wasted my time and life only for him to tell me that I am not his dream woman?

Little Dingaling

I broke it off with my boyfriend of ten years because he wouldn't marry me. So, I made him my plan B guy. I met another guy shortly after, and he is sweet and all. But he has a little dingaling. And I'm seriously thinking about leaving him and going back to my plan B guy. I cannot do a little dingaling!

Tree Years a Virgin

Let me just go ahead and tell you the truth; I stayed with my ex-boyfriend for almost ten years because the sex was out of this world. I was still a virgin when I met my boyfriend. He was my first and my everything. But, before that, I held out for three years in hopes that he would marry me. I wanted him to take it to a new level and put a ring on it. Finally, I gave it up because I was head over heels in love with him. So, once I hit 30, and he still didn't ask me to marry him, I bailed. I refuse to waste another ten years of my life.

15 Years a Girlfriend

Brand New Bed

For 13 years, I stayed with my boyfriend. But often, I move in and out of his place. He promised me that we were going to get married and settle down over the years. One day I came home early because I was not feeling well. Would you believe that no good piece of crap was screwing my best friend on my brand-new bed!?

So, I kicked him and her out. Unfortunately, I was not feeling well because I was pregnant with our third baby. I decided to move on with my life for the sake of our kids and me. I haven't been in a committed relationship since no one has been worthy of my time.

Liar Liar, Not a Promise Keeper

I have been with my boyfriend for 14 years. And he has promised me that he would marry me. But instead of marrying me, my boyfriend has cheated throughout our relationship. Not only has he cheated, but he had a new woman every week. I was so pissed that he would disrespect me like that. One day, I finally accepted that he was a liar because he never kept his promise to marry me. So, one weekend, while he was at one of his other women's houses, I packed mine and the kids' stuff and left. That lying behind man was married in less than two years.

Engaged After Ten Years

I dated my fiancé for ten years before he finally asked me to marry him. He has made it clear he didn't want anyone else throughout our relationship. He always tells me that he loves me. My fiancé and I have lived together, bought a house, and saved money for our future. Five years later, I'm still waiting for him to set a date to get married. How long does it take to set a date to get married? Now, after all this time, my fiancé is asking why get married when we are practically married?

Nest Egg for His Wife and Kids

I've been with my boyfriend since college. We are both in our mid-30s. We've lived all these years separately, even though I think we could save money by living together. When I talk to him about marriage, he said he's not ready because he's working hard to pay off his two houses and build a nest egg for his wife and kids. I love that about him that he plans. But how long will it take for him to marry me? Now I'm wondering if he's ever going to marry me.

Please See My Worth

I feel so hopeless. After sixteen years and seven kids, my baby daddy has yet to marry me. I want to leave, but where am I going with seven children? Plus, I can't afford to live on my own. I just wish my boyfriend would see my worth and make an honest woman out of me.

I Don't Mind Waiting

I don't see the big deal in waiting for a man to be ready to marry me. I have been with my boyfriend since I was 14 and he was 16. And not once did we break up or be with other people. It's been 15 years, and I'm still waiting for my boyfriend to propose. He said he isn't ready, and that's cool with me. I don't mind waiting for my boyfriend to be ready to marry me. When he's ready to get married, I'll be right here along with our kids.

Love is More than a Piece of Paper

I have waited over 13 years for my boyfriend to ask me to marry him. To me, love is more than a ring and a piece of paper. I love my boyfriend with all my heart. And I'm cool with what we have going on here. My boyfriend will ask me to marry him when he's ready.

Getting Impatient

My boyfriend and I started dating when I was eighteen, and he was twenty-four. I'm now thirty; he's thirty-six, and he still ain't asked me to marry him yet. My boyfriend finished school, and his business is doing great. I just don't understand what's taking him such a long time to ask me to marry him. I am getting impatient.

Lapdog

This COVID 19 pandemic has helped me see that I don't know my baby daddy of fourteen years. Because of Covid-19, we've been home, and he avoids me at every cost. I just want to be all up underneath him. But he says I'm following him around like a little lapdog.

A lapdog? I told my boyfriend that if he doesn't make me his wife, I will be leaving after the virus. And he said he couldn't wait for the virus to be over. What the heck he means by that?

I'm Ready Now

Fourteen years, four kids, a whole lot of debt, and many vehicles later, I am finally ready to leave my baby daddy. I feel like a fool for having all these kids for my baby daddy without him marrying me. Now I must start over because I let this fool waste half of my life.

Oh Death, where is Your Sting

I stayed with my boyfriend for fifteen years, waiting for him to marry me. My boyfriend told me that he couldn't marry me until his mother dies. What? My boyfriend can't marry me until his mother passes? Well, the light came on for me when I learned that his mother is a healthy 55-year-old woman. I packed mine and the children's stuff and left that lying fool.

My Boyfriend and His Wife

Five years ago, my fourteen-year boyfriend surprised me with a beautiful and romantic Valentine's Day dinner. He told me that he finally decided to divorce his wife so that he could marry me. But my boyfriend still has not asked me to marry him. What do you think is taking him such a long time?

A House Under My Nose

After twelve years together and three kids, my babies' daddy told me that we'd grown apart and should go our separate ways. I thought I was having a nightmare when he told me he thinks we'd grown apart. How is that possible? We've been a perfect and happy family. For years I worked two jobs and took care of us when my baby daddy wasn't working. I helped him get a decent job, and he was making good money. The nerve of this fool!

Shortly after he told me that we'd grown apart, he moved out of our two-bedroom apartment into a house. At first, I thought he rented it, but then come to find out, he bought it. How did he buy a house under my nose without me knowing? When I asked him to put my name on the deed, he said we're not married. So, I asked him when he would marry me, and he said he wasn't ready to get married.

What's the Cost?

My boyfriend and I have been together for 14 years. All these years, I've asked him when was he going to marry me? But he always made excuses for why he can't marry me. For example, my boyfriend said he would marry me when his money was right. But the one he used all the time was that he wasn't financially ready. How was he not ready financially when he works two jobs? But I earn more, so I pay most of the bills?

So, I am sure he should have enough money saved up to marry me by now. What is he waiting on to marry me? How much money does it take? I told him that I would be okay with a ring from a second-hand store, and we could get married at the courthouse. I just want us to get married and keep our family together.

Ticking Clock

My boyfriend and I were best friends and lovers for eight years. When I got pregnant, he proposed. Now, we've been engaged for seven years. And to date, he hasn't mentioned anything about getting married.

Every time I ask my fiancé when are we getting married, he says it's just a matter of time and money. I don't know how much longer it will take because I want us to have at least two more kids. Plus, my clock is ticking!

My Boyfriend's Brother

My boyfriend and I have been together for almost 15 years. He keeps giving me the run around about when he's gonna marry me. He has told me every excuse in the book. Recently, I found out that my boyfriend's little brother is getting married. His brother has only dated his girlfriend for a year and a half. I am so pissed at my stupid boyfriend because he keeps saying he's not ready. How could his baby brother be ready to marry a girl he met a year ago, but this grown fool is not ready yet? After four kids and all this time, he is still not ready? What does he need to be ready to marry me?

Tomorrow Is Not Promised

A month after my boyfriend and I met, he asked to move in with me. I agreed because he said he planned to propose to me in a year. I told him from the beginning that I wanted to get married. After almost thirteen years together, I asked him how come he hasn't married me yet. He told me that he had purchased my ring and planned to propose. After two more years, I asked how long it would take for him to ask me to be his wife.

Sadly, not long after that, he was killed in a drive-by shooting. I wasted 13 years with a man, and when he died, I got nothing. I couldn't even afford to pay the rent because he was the breadwinner while I took care of our kids. My kids couldn't even get Survival Benefits because he was "working" under the table.

Run

I gave my baby daddy 15 years of my life and four kids. I am still waiting for him to marry me. But, three months ago, I overheard him telling his mother that he wouldn't marry me. So, I packed up the kids and myself and ran. The nerve of my baby daddy saying he wouldn't marry me! After he promised all those years that he would marry me. I want to get married, no need for me to waste any more time waiting for him to marry me.

Too Expensive

After fifteen years, my baby daddy finally proposed. We took our engagement pictures, had a little party and everything. I put the first down payment on the hall, and he was to pay the next one. To my surprised, when I called the venue to check how things were going, I learned that my baby daddy never made the next payment.

So, I asked him what happened, and he said he's not at peace with going through with the wedding. And that it was too expensive.

Too expensive? After fifteen years of my life, time, and four kids, a lovely reception is too expensive? I wasted all this money to get ready for my big day, and this fool broke it off.

Side Chick

I've been with my boyfriend for 16 years. Foolishly, I was one of his side chicks. I was stupid to think that we would be married by now. Every time I bring up marriage, he gets aggressive and says he will never get married again. But I told him when we got together that I wanted to get married. He said he would leave his wife to marry me. But we've been together longer than he was married, and he still hasn't married me yet.

I Can't Believe It

My boyfriend and I have been together for about 16 years. I sat down to talk to him about us moving in together, getting married, and adding a few more kids to our family. I have a child from a previous relationship. I was shocked to learn that he doesn't want to have any more kids or get married. I couldn't believe it! I asked him why he didn't tell me all this before, and he said he did. Honestly, I don't remember him ever telling me that he doesn't want to get married or have kids.

During our 16 years, it didn't bother me because I was busy working on my master's and paying off my student loans.

But now that I'm finished with school and in my early 30s, I'm ready to get married and have more children. So, I just basically wasted almost 20 years of my life with my childhood sweetheart.

Time

My fiancé proposed to me on his 40th birthday after we've been together for five years. Sadly, he passed suddenly, at forty-eight. He always said we would have a big, beautiful wedding when the time was right. That time never came. I feel so lost without my fiancé. How do I start over after all these years?

Dream Dreamer

Fifteen years, lots of dreams, and three babies later, my baby daddy, best friend, and the love of my life has still not married me. But for some reason, he's been telling me to get my heads out of the clouds. Also, he told me to stop dreaming about getting married because not every couple must get married. What the heck is he talking about? I always told him that I wanted to get married. So, after almost twenty years, he's telling me that not all couples should get married?

On and Off

I've been with my man for fifteen years on and off. Every time we broke up, it was because he didn't follow through with asking me to marry him. And I just got tired of empty promises for fifteen years. Also, we broke up because he cheated a few times. I have always wanted to get married for years. And I told him from day one that I wanted to get married. So, this is not news to him. I'm getting sick and tired of the back and forth; he has yet to ask me to marry me. Or else the next time we break up, that will be it.

Waiting for Him to Be Ready

For 16 years, I have been waiting for my boyfriend to marry me. I'm 35 years old, and I'm ready to have more kids. My clock has been ticking for a few years now—we have one child together, and I want to have more. I love him so much and want to spend the rest of my life with him, but he said he isn't ready to get married yet. When I asked him when he would be ready to get married, he said he didn't know. How much longer do I need to wait for him to be ready?

Wanting the Same Thing

I got pregnant in my last year of college. I gave birth a week before graduation, and I was expecting a proposal from my boyfriend. I have always told him that I wanted to get married. Fourteen years and four kids later, and he hasn't brought up marriage. In the beginning, I thought that we wanted the same things, but in the end, it's evident that he doesn't want the same things as me. I hate to split up our happy home with our kids, but I have always wanted to get married. I'm not sure if I can stick around any longer, hoping and praying that he will marry me.

Stepping out on Faith

My boyfriend and I have been together for 14 years. Right about now, I'm getting antsy about when is he gonna ask me to marry him. So, I'm going to step out on faith and buy my engagement ring. I don't want anything too expensive. I sent him some pictures asking him which one he would pick for me. Would you believe my boyfriend of fourteen years asked me why I was sending him engagement ring pictures? I told him because it's time for him to marry me. He asked me if he ever told me he would marry me? I told him, "The "curse word" you will! Because it's been almost 14 years, and we have four kids together."

If He Wants to Or Not

After ten years with my baby daddy, I stopped counting how long I've been waiting for him to marry me. However, we've been together for about fifteen years. So, I told my boyfriend that we're getting married next year whether he wants to or not. To date, he has yet to propose. Maybe we will just skip that part?

30th Birthday Present

I met my boyfriend when I was fourteen years old in high school. We had our first baby at 16. He promised that we would get married as soon as we got older. Sixteen years later, I have spent more than half my life with my boyfriend, and he still hasn't asked me to marry him. I invested so much in my boyfriend and our relationship.

It was only for him to leave me right before I turned thirty for the woman he is married to now. What was so special about her and not me? I am still in shock and disbelief because my boyfriend is all I've known. He is the only man I've been with, and I just knew that we would have gotten married.

20 Years a Girlfriend

Repent

At almost forty-five years old, I'm sitting here, thinking over my life and all the wasted time, energy, and years trying to build men up. And, at the same time, hoping that one day, one of them would appreciate and love me enough to marry me and make me their prize. In every relationship, I went the extra mile. I was the perfect homemaker and cook. Plus, my bedroom' skill was top of the line. The men would always come back for more. I spent my money if they didn't have it.

I made them feel special, and I committed and was exclusive with every man. Then, at forty, a light came on for me when I heard the word "repent." Repent means to turn and go in the opposite direction. So, I decided to stop being a foolish woman by investing in every man I met. Finally, I realized I should allow men to find me and choose me. So that is what I did, and in less than three years, I got married to the most wonderful man, my husband, Edward.

Meet Me at City Hall

My boyfriend and I have been together since college. I have always told him that I wanted to get married. We have three kids together and wonderful life. My fortieth birthday is coming up, and I want us to get married. So, I told my boyfriend that I would no longer shack up and have sex with him. I also told him to meet me at City hall on our anniversary, or else we would be over! He never showed up, and I was so embarrassed. All my family and friends were outside, and this man I gave all my best years to didn't show up for me. By the time I got back home, he had moved out. How could he do me like that? What about our family?

Old and Washed Up

Twenty years and three sons later, I gave my kids father, only for him to get up and marry a woman 15 years my junior! I told him that he's going through a midlife crisis, and he said I was just jealous. My sons' father also said that I am washed up and old, and he couldn't grow old with me. I still don't understand how he could walk away from twenty years with the boys and me?

Cross Country

I stayed in a relationship for eighteen years, hoping that my boyfriend would ask me to be his wife one day. I recently decided to pack up my stuff and move across the country to get away from him. I knew that I would run back to him if I stayed in our state because I love him so much. Now he wants me and our kids to move back home. He promised that we would get married this time. I want to get married, so I'm thinking about going back home.

I'm Starting to Believe Him

I am fifty-five years old. I was with my boyfriend for almost twenty years. I don't know why I sat there and allowed time to pass by. And, at nearly sixty years old, my boyfriend still has not mentioned marrying me. Sometimes, I think that we're way too old to be playing house. My boyfriend said if it isn't broke, why try to fix it? At this point, I'm starting to believe him. Our kids are out of the home and away to college. Is it worth it to start over now?

Black Folks Don't Do Counseling

Since the age of 18, I've been in many different relationships with various boyfriends. For my 30th birthday, my gift to myself was to get rid of all my boyfriends and be single for a while. I feel as if all my boyfriends damaged me. Also, I've been so disappointed that none of them married me. I keep bouncing from one relationship to another, looking for a man to love and appreciate me. So, I am thinking of going to counseling to work on some of these issues. Yea, I know counseling is taboo for black folks, but I feel as if I need it. I think something is definitely wrong with me.

Deadline

Twenty years I wasted with my kids' father. I got pregnant because we had unprotected sex on the first date. I rushed into having sex, and I take full responsibility now that I'm looking back. I promised myself that I would never waste all my precious time with a man who refuses to marry me. I've been with my new boyfriend for five years now; if he doesn't ask me to marry him by the end of this year, then I'm leaving. When I asked him, what's taking him so long to marry him, he said he's not ready. Well, how long does it take for a man to be ready to get married?

Proposal Negotiation

For almost twenty years, I've been with my baby daddy, and we have three kids. I think twenty years is more than enough time for a man to be ready to get married. Recently, I asked my baby daddy what does he need to propose to me? He asked me why I sounded desperate to get married and negotiate a proposal from him. I have begged for us to go to the courthouse, and I told him that the stones in my ring don't have to be real. I just want us to get married. Does it take all of that to get a man to marry you?

Introductions

I have been introducing my boyfriend to friends and family for over twenty years. And I am so sick and tired of it. When is he going to marry me? When will I be able to say this is my husband? Gosh, I just thought he would ask me to marry me by now.

Side Chick?

After eighteen years, I finally built up enough nerve to tell my boyfriend that I wasn't happy and wanted to get married. I told him that if he didn't marry me, I didn't want to be in a relationship with him anymore. He promised me that he was gonna marry me when he gets some money. Then this idiot had the nerve to cheat on me and made two outside kids. Every time he cheated on me, I felt like I was the side chick.

Love's Gone

After twenty years, my boyfriend finally started to do right. He got a decent job and stopped drinking and cheating. But I realized that the love I had for him was gone. Right now, I'm wondering how to tell him I don't want to be with him anymore without an argument. The truth is I wished I had left when I had a thousand reasons. The crazy thing is, though, my boyfriend still hasn't asked me to marry him after twenty years.

Go Ahead Then

I was with my boyfriend for over 20 years, waiting for him to marry me. After four kids, many wasted years and time, I finally realized that he would never marry me. When I put my foot down and told him that he should marry me or I was going to leave, he told me to go ahead then. The light came on for me that he didn't love me. After 20 years, this man told me to go? I was mad, bitter, and angry for a long time! But the truth is, I had no-one to be upset with but myself. He did what I allowed; he threw me away like I was trash.

Love & Respect

For twenty-two years, I was with my boyfriend. And we shacked up for twenty years. This man cheated and lied every chance he got. My boyfriend still didn't marry me through all the lying and cheating. But I decided to stick it through because I loved him so much. I gave this man twenty-two years of my life, and what did he do? My boyfriend cheated on me again and got a whole baby. I tried to stay after, but I just couldn't do it. I feel like, after twenty-two years, he should have more than enough love and respect for me to keep it in his pants. And to get some chick knocked up? Oh no!

Not His Wife

I asked my boyfriend of over twenty years why he doesn't have me on his social media—no pictures or mention. He posts our kids on his social media all the time. But he has not posted anything about me or even a hint that I'm his woman or the mother of his children. Not only does he not mention me on social media, but it makes me angry that my boyfriend likes other women's pictures and puts emojis and hearts on them.

So, I asked my boyfriend why he hasn't posted any pictures of me or us. Girl, this fool boyfriend says it's because I'm not his wife. And the only woman he will mention on his social media is his wife. So, I asked him when he was gonna marry me, and he shook his head and walked out of the room. I don't know what to do. It's hard starting over after twenty years. Twenty years of my life, I gave this fool!

Golden Years

I just found out that my boyfriend of eighteen years has been cheating on me for the last two years. My boyfriend is sixty-three, and I am sixty years old. I cannot believe he is doing me like that. He didn't marry me all these years, but he's cheating on me? What else can a man be looking for at sixty-three years old? The sad thing is, even though he cheated, I am still hoping that we would get married and ride off in the sunset and spend our golden years together forever. At sixty years old, I should not be worried about marriage.

Proving to Him

When I met my boyfriend, I was just graduating with my master's in social work. He was just starting medical school, so I let him move in with me. And I told him that I wanted to get married. Sadly I allowed him to move in with me. And I wanted to prove to him that I was supportive. I even took a part-time job so that he didn't have to work but concentrate on school instead. Once he finished his residency and started to work, he left me and married another girl that didn't even have a bachelor's degree.

Still Learning

My boyfriend and I have been together for ten years. Then I told him if he didn't propose to me, I was gonna pack up our five kids and move back home to my father's house. So, my boyfriend proposed to me, and it's been another ten years. I finally left him after it was obvious that he wasn't gonna marry me. When I asked my boyfriend why he wasted twenty years of my life waiting for him to marry me, he said he was still learning how to treat a woman correctly.

No Thanks

I was with my kids' father for twenty years. When I finally had enough of his bull crap and decided to move on, then he wanted to propose to me. I told him no thanks. Then I moved out and left him with the mortgage that he can't pay alone. I just don't understand why it took him that long to want to marry me. And now that he realized that he was gonna lose me, he wants to try and hold on to me? No, thank you!

Will You Marry Me?

After seventeen years, I got tired of asking my boyfriend when he was gonna marry me. So, I decided to ask him to marry me. Shockingly, he said no. He said it's a man's place to ask a woman to be his wife. I asked him why he hasn't asked me, and he said he's just not ready to get married yet.

From Boyfriend to Wonderful Man

I wasted 20 years with my college sweetheart. For years I begged him to marry me. I finally left him, but guess what? Two years after I left that fool of a man, I met the most wonderful man who married me in a year and a half. I often think about what would have happened if I didn't leave my boyfriend. I would have missed out on a wonderful man who loves me enough to marry me.

Marriage is Overrated

I was with my guy for 19 years. I got tired of asking him to marry me, so I stopped. One day he told me that he doesn't understand why I want to get married so much. He went on to say that marriage is overrated, and why would I want to mess up a stable relationship?

40th Birthday Present

For 19 years, I wasted my life and time waiting and thinking that my boyfriend would finally commit and marry me. To my disappointment, he never proposed and continued to be a playboy. So, for my 40th birthday, I decided to give myself freedom from that fool. I packed my stuff and left, and in no time, I met my awesome husband, who proposed in less than a year. It kills me that I wasted all that time waiting for a man I wanted to love me, but he never did.

Free Milk

I played wifey for 18 years, washing, cooking, cleaning, and having my boyfriend's babies. Finally, I came to my senses that I was with someone who didn't want me to begin with. I often laugh at myself when my grandmother would always say, "why should he buy the cow when he can get the milk for free?" Now I'm almost 40 years old, single, with four kids from a deadbeat. Unfortunately, I wasted half of my life learning a valuable lesson. If a man wants you, he will pursue and marry you. Also, I realized that nothing would make a man want to marry me, him if he's not ready.

25 Years a Girlfriend

Who's Gonna Want Me?

My childhood sweetheart and I have been together since high school. Twenty-five years and five kids later, I am still waiting for him to marry me.

What am I supposed to do? I might as well wait it out. Who's gonna want me with five kids and no stable work history?

In Sickness and in Health

My boyfriend and I have been together since I was 13. I am 42 years old now, and he still has not married me. I don't understand it at all. Why hasn't he married me yet? I've been with him through thick and thin, in sickness and in health. When we lost everything and had to move in with my mom, we stuck together. Yet, he has not asked me to be his wife. I don't get it at all!

No Desire

For 24 years, I was with my boyfriend and begged him to marry me. Then he was diagnosed with cancer, so he proposed. It's crazy how much I wanted to marry him, but I had no desire to when he finally proposed. I felt like he didn't want to marry me, but because he was sick and had no other options, he needed a forever caretaker. So, I decided to move out after he was in remission.

What You Want

My high school sweetheart and I have been together for 24 years. About a month ago, I asked him how come we never got married. He said he was not ready to get married and give me what I wanted. How is it possible that after 24 years, this man is not ready to get married? So, I asked him what about now, and he said it doesn't make sense to get married after all of these years.

Toxicity

My boyfriend and I have been together for 25 years. Lately, our relationship has gotten so toxic. Now we're always fighting and arguing. And most of the time, my boyfriend leaves because of our fights. Then he stays away for up to three days at a time. I cannot even stand to see him, and his voice makes me want to vomit! I have lots of resentment towards him that he hasn't married me yet. I think maybe we need to take a break.

Haven't Got Around to It

My boyfriend and I have been together for 25 years. I have always wanted to get married. But my boyfriend has always said he wasn't sure if he wanted to get married. However, my boyfriend said he would think about getting married since I want to get married. Although my boyfriend and I have the marriage talk all the time, he still has not asked me to marry him. So basically, I've been planning a wedding without a proposal. When I asked him, what's taking him such a long time to marry me, he said he's been busy and hasn't gotten around to it. Twenty-five years, and he hasn't gotten around to marrying me?

Giving My Boyfriend a Husband's Privileges

I played the wifey role for twenty-five years only because I thought he saw a future with me. But It took me realizing that I'm only ten years away from retirement to realize that I had wasted half of my life with a boyfriend. A boyfriend that I gave husband privileges to without the covenant of marriage. And when I think about it, I guess I was trying to prove to him that I was wifey material.

Marriage Would Ruin It

I don't understand why y'all want to get married. My parents have been together for 25 years and are not married. For my parents, I think married would ruin their relationship. My mom said that it is the best and happiest relationship she has ever had. So, I'm not gonna press my boyfriend to marry me because we are good. If not getting married worked for my mom, it will work for me. Marriage might ruin our relationship. And if my boyfriend wants to marry me, he will. But he will not be getting any pressure from me.

Over 30 Years a Girlfriend

Engaged but Still Not Married

My boyfriend and I were together for 16 years before he popped the question. To celebrate, he took me to a fancy restaurant. He has never taken me anywhere like that before. We have been engaged for 13 years now. It's starting to bug me that we haven't gotten married yet. After almost 30 years of being with my boyfriend, I'm beginning to have regrets.

Happy

Big daddy and I have been together for so long that it's as if we're married. Oh, sure, it still bothers me that we haven't gotten married, but we are happy other than a piece of paper. Twenty-nine years on and off, breakups and makeups, kids here and there, and then COVID-19 happened.

He had nowhere else to go, so he asked me if he could move back in with the kids and me. He cooked a nice meal, and then he finally asked me to marry him. Even though my now fiancé didn't have a ring, I am so happy that he finally sees my worth and wants to make an honest woman out of me!

Over 40 Years a Girlfriend

My Married Boyfriend

I've been with my married boyfriend for 40 years. Even though he was married, I believe that he would eventually leave her. Finally, she kicked him out, and he drove for two days to come down south and asked me to marry him. We went to Walmart and picked out a nice ring. Now, I'm just waiting for him to divorce his wife so that we can get married!

45 Years a Girlfriend

Recently on the news, there was a story of a man who was with his girlfriend for forty-five years. They had built a life together for all those years.

One day, they had a huge fight, and the girlfriend told her boyfriend that she was done with the relationship. She also threatened to put him out of their home. His whole life flashed before him, and then he gave in. After forty-five years, the boyfriend finally broke down and proposed to his girlfriend. I don't know about you, but I wonder how long they will be engaged for. Lol!

How to Know if You Have a Shut-Up Ring

I would love to hear your thoughts about all these women who have been waiting a lifetime for their boyfriends and or baby daddies to marry them. Some of you ladies might have read *10 Years a Girlfriend* up to this part and think it doesn't apply to you because you have a ring on your finger.

So, here's a question, how long has it been that your boyfriend or baby daddy proposed to you? Did you set a date? It doesn't take forever to get married. Once he proposed, you should have been married six months to a year later.

Are you sure you don't have a shut-up ring? What's a shut-up ring, you might ask? My sister, I'm sorry to tell you this, but you might just have a shut-up ring. I didn't know what a shut-up ring was until a few years ago.

A while back, I was at work when a gentleman commented on my rings. For those of you who think you can nag a man into marrying you. Our conversation went something like this:

Him: That's a nice ring.

Me: Thank you.

Him: Looks expensive.

Me: I'm an expensive woman.

Him: He must really love you.

Me: He does.

Him: He must really value you.

Me: He does, and when you value someone, you will show them you value them.

Him: **S**ugar, **H**oney, **I**ced Tea, I was thinking of going to Kmart.

Me: looking up at him, said: Kmart?

Him: Man, I'm just trying to shut her up.

Me: Do you love her?

Him: hmmm?

Me: Do you value her?

Him: Guess not.

Me: Are you gonna marry her?

Him: Nope.

Me: Why not?

Him: She ain't the one.

Me: So, why are you gonna give her a ring?

Him: So, she can shut the heck up! I just want her to shut up about me marrying her.

Me: CLUTCHED MY PEARLS!!

Ladies, when you force a man to marry you, what you will get is a shut-up ring. When you beg and plead for him to marry you, he will give you a shut-up ring. When he gives you a ring without a wedding date six months to a year later, you might just have a shut-up ring.

Have there been couples that have been engaged forever and eventually got married? Yes, but we are not about wasting years of our time and lives waiting for a man to marry us, ladies.

Here are a few testimonials of engaged women and how long they have been waiting:

- One year together and eight engaged.
- Two years dated, engaged for fifteen.
- Six years together and engaged for five.
- Seven years of dating and engaged for six years.
- Eight years together, engaged for ten.

- Nine years together and engaged for eight.
- Ten years dated, engaged for ten.
- Eleven years together and engaged three.
- Twelve years together and engaged for five.
- Fourteen years dated, engaged for five.
- Fifteen years together and engaged for three.
- Fifteen years dated and engaged for seven.
- Twenty years dated and engaged five.

Do You Have the Girlfriend Spirit?

Did you know that everything has a spirit? Have you heard of the fruit of the spirit? **Galatians 5 22 But the fruit of the Spirit is love, joy, peace, longsuffering, gentleness, goodness, faith, 23 Meekness, temperance: against such there is no law.**

24 And they that are Christ's have crucified the flesh with the affections and lusts.25 If we live in the Spirit, let us also walk in the Spirit. 26 Let us not be desirous of vain glory, provoking one another, envying one another.

Christian women often refer to themselves as virtuous women. But the Virtuous Woman also has a spirit. Young Esther was able to win the king over because of her spirit. Delilah was able to get Samson to tell her all his heart because of her spirit. There is a spirit of a wife, as there is a spirit of the Church. And it is essential to know which spirit you are walking in.

Likewise, there is a spirit of girlfriends. The girlfriend spirit is of the spirit of Jezebel. Who was Jezebel? She was a princess whose father, King of the Zidonians, was a weak man and king. Jezebel's weak father married her off to another weak and feminine man, King Ahab. Therefore, Jezebel had to become masculine and in charge.

King Ahab once cried to Jezebel about a vineyard he wanted. Jezebel killed the vineyard owner and gave it to her lil boy husband. In another instance, when the Prophet Elijah killed Baal's prophets, Jezebel threatened to kill Elijah.

The Prophet Elijah was so scared of Queen Jezebel that he ran and hid. He became extremely depressed; he wanted to die. The spirit of a girlfriend is one that says, "*You are going to marry me, no matter what. So, what if you do not want to marry me? I have been sexing, washing, cooking, and cleaning; therefore, YOU MUST MARRY ME!"*

However, on the other hand, the spirit of a wife says, *"I will choose a husband from the men that find me. I will marry the man who has gone through the process to profess his love, provide a comfortable life for me, and protect my children and me."*

Ladies, if you possess the spirit of girlfriends, it is time for you to get delivered in Jesus' name. Aren't you tired of being a girlfriend to every man you meet? Aren't you tired of building up several boyfriends only for them to leave you and find a woman who can appreciate them for the man you build them into?

Why I Have Never Had a Boyfriend

Would you believe that I have never had a boyfriend? Are you shocked? Did you pick your mouth up off the floor yet? Nope, I have never had a boyfriend because I do not believe in boyfriends. Why? My father in the faith taught us that "girlfriend and boyfriend" are not in the Bible.

My father went on to say that If I wanted to get married, I needed to carry myself like a wife and believe in God for a husband.

And so, at the ripe age of 35, I finally got married. In the meantime, I knew many women who were in their mid-thirties, divorced, and looking for husband number two.

Additionally, I knew many women who were also in their mid-thirties, shacking up with their boyfriends with a house, several kids, joint bank accounts, and the like, waiting for their boyfriends to marry them.

As for me, I think 35 is way too old to be getting married for the first time. Many women are grandmothers at 35. But during those years of singleness, I refused to have boyfriends because I wanted a husband.

Now, to the unwise, this makes no sense. How do you become a wife if you are not a man's girlfriend first? Many have even asked if my now-husband was not my boyfriend. Nope! He was never my boyfriend. Why sign up for a girlfriend when I was a wife?

To me, it makes no sense to meet a man, get into a relationship, and hope that one day he would marry me. Instead, it is crucial to date, aka gather data about guys without committing. Learn about them to see if they match up with what you want in a husband and if you're what they want in a wife.

After completing *10 Years a Girlfriend*, I asked my husband if he remembered what I said to him when he asked me about being exclusive. He said I told him that I did not believe in boyfriends. Also, he said to himself, "Oh, oh."

So, while I was dating my husband, I continued to accept dates from other guys. But eight months after that, my husband proposed and wanted to get married two months later. However, we got married the following May, as I said no to getting married too quickly.

Why Boyfriends are like Gambling

When I tell people that I do not believe in boyfriends, I get the push back that so and so was together with her boyfriend forever, and they finally got married. Or so and so were boyfriend and girlfriend throughout college, and they eventually got married.

Well, of course—that is how the enemy works. Surprisingly, many of these boyfriends and girlfriends profess Christ while participating in a counterfeit marriage and, yes, fornication.

There will be some girlfriends and boyfriends who will get married. That gives many women hope that if they get a boyfriend and stick it out with them, they will finally get married. But that is a huge gamble, don't you think?

Think about the lottery. How many people win? Think about the casinos. How many people who go into the casinos leave with winnings? No, most people lose their money, which is how the casinos become rich. And likewise for the lottery. But some people will win to give other people hope that, if they play, they might have a chance of winning.

Lovelies, boyfriends are like temporary fixtures—why gamble with your life, time, and eggs, hoping that this one man that you love and want so much will marry you?

Why You Should Never Put All Your Eggs in One Basket

The saying "never putting all of your eggs in one basket is" near and dear to my heart. My grandmother taught it to me at around three or four years old. You see, my grandmother raised chickens. I remember as if it was yesterday, going to the chicken coop to pick up the eggs.

My grandmother, who we affectionately call Mama, would give me a bowl and one for my brother. And she would say, "Never put all of your eggs in one basket because if it falls, then all of the eggs will break, and we won't have anything for breakfast."

In dating, the never put all your eggs in one basket concept is vital. Millions of single women meet men, set their eyes on them, and tell themselves; *this man will marry me*. These women who want to get married waste years, hoping, building with these men, shacking up, having babies, with fingers crossed that these men would marry them.

It is only for many men to get up and leave their girlfriends or baby mommas and their children and marry other women in no time. These women are left broken-hearted and disappointed with a whole lot of baggage because they put all their marital hopes and dreams in one man's flimsy, possibly full of holes, basket.

The Boyfriend Seed

A boyfriend and girlfriend relationship are a counterfeit of God's plan for marriage. It is a fake title of God's intention for one man and one woman. Shacking up is also a counterfeit of the covenant of marriage. Yet, having a boyfriend is like a badge of honor in many circles. Exceedingly early in a young girl's life, the boyfriend seed is planted.

Boyfriend and girlfriend are fake titles, where couples live like they are married while wanting the benefits of being married. While many couples say marriage is just a piece of paper, deep down on the inside, they want the benefits of that piece of paper.

From the time we are babies, people asked if we have a boyfriend yet. I see it even with my little boy, who is currently in preschool, with moms of little girls asking their daughters to be my baby boy's girlfriend. Of course, I am quick to jump in and say, "Oh no, we don't do boyfriends and girlfriends."

I have even had one mom tell me that we should hook our kids up while they are young so that when they get older, they will be together. You see, I do not believe in boyfriends, period! I do not believe in kids having boyfriends, and I do not believe in planting the boyfriend seed. I believe in preparing my kids to be husbands and wives.

Boyfriends are not in the Bible, and I think, the same way we prepare our kids to be presidents, doctors, lawyers, teachers, police officers, and servicemen and women, we need to prepare our babies to be husbands and wives. The same way we are to prepare them for eternity.

Now, will our kids say they have boyfriends and girlfriends? Yes, they will—however, my point is that we need to prepare them to be husbands and wives. I talk to them about Adam and Eve and all the beautiful couples in the Bible who got married. Preparing our children to be husbands and wives takes constant work and diligence.

Also, **Proverbs 22:6** encourages us to **raise a child in the way they should go, and when they are old, they will not depart from it.** So, mommies, if we can plant the boyfriend and girlfriend seed, then why not plant the husband and wife seed and raise your children in that manner?

If the boyfriend seed has been planted in the hearts of your children, please root it out now before it is too late. Settling for being a girlfriend when God called us wives is living beneath our privileges.

And we don't have time to get emotionally involved with various men waiting for them to marry us.

In the meantime, we drop the panties and pop babies out for these males who don't even love us enough to marry us. How many ladies do you know who have had multiple babies with every man they laid down with?

Why Is Marriage NOT a Goal?

MARRIAGE IS AND SHOULD BE A GOAL! Yes, I said marriage is a goal, and I will not back down from it. If 70% of black women are chronically single, meaning they are not and will not get married, why *shouldn't* marriage be a goal? Why is everything else a goal and not marriage?

Think of several achievements that we call goals. Going to school, getting our degrees, buying our first home or a new car are all goals. Traveling the world, saving an emergency fund, buying a $1,200 pair of shoes and $13,000 purses are all goals. But when it comes to marriage, "OH NO, MARRIAGE IS NOT A GOAL?"

Women of color are becoming the most educated group of women. We have big jobs, getting more and more accomplished than our ancestors and our male counterparts. **HOWEVER, WE ARE THE MOST SINGLE GROUP OF WOMEN!!** I will be writing more about the high number of single black women, but I just wanted to drop this little shocker about the high number of single black women here and now. And **YES, LADIES, MARRIAGE IS AND SHOULD BE A GOAL TO YOU IF YOU WANT TO GET MARRIED!**

Many women waste years of their lives on various boyfriends, waiting for the men to marry them. Wasting precious time with males they want to marry, but who don't see their girlfriends like Christ sees the Church. My sisters, you need to set your eyes on the covenant, protection, and provision of marriage if that's what you want.

My sisters, if you want to get married, then **MARRIAGE IS AND SHOULD BE A GOAL!!** So please work on accomplishing your marital goal. Beloved, if marriage is what you want, then set your eyes, heart, mind, soul, and spirit on the covenant of marriage. Don't shack up and waste time with boyfriends. Don't procreate with men who have not gone through the process to profess their love, to provide for and protect you, aka husbands.

When you do things God's way, you are paving the way for you and your children to have what God intended for you. Sisters, it is your responsibility to live your lives according to what you want. Having marriage as a goal mindset if you want to be married is not about making marriage an idol. Making marriage an idol is a lie many have used to keep us single.

However, the marriage mindset is about living your life God's way. Marriage mindset is about learning to choose the **BEST HUSBAND** for you and father for your children. It's about living your life as a wife and a virtuous woman. When you have a marriage mindset, you will not allow men to use your body for sex and procreation.

The marriage mindset is about dating for marriage only. The marriage mindset is about not shacking up. Having a marriage mindset is about not wasting years of your life with men who want to use you as a preparer to prepare themselves for the next woman.

Think about it. How many stories have you heard about women spending years of their lives waiting for their boyfriends to marry them? Only for those men to up and leave those women and marry other women in a year? The marriage mindset is about changing the statistics and choosing a better life for ourselves and our children.

My husband's mother told him and his siblings not to have any kids outside of the covenant of marriage. Guess what? None of them did. My husband was in his mid-forties when we met, with no kids, and had never been married. His mother taught him not to have any kids out of wedlock, and he listened to her wise words.

Many in the Church and within the black community have been bashed when we talk about getting married. The Church tells us that we should "Seek first the kingdom of heaven." And to them, seeking God's kingdom means being in the Church every time its doors are open. If we took any time to date or made ourselves available to be found, then we wouldn't be seeking God's kingdom.

In the black community, we are told to get our degrees and big jobs, so we don't have to depend on a man (aka our husbands) to care for us. After all, **WE ARE STRONG, INDEPENDENT BLACK WOMEN, AND WE DON'T NEED MEN**. My sisters, the strong independent black woman who doesn't need a man/husband mindset, is all lies and traps from the devil to keep us single and husbandless.

Meanwhile, our churches and communities are filled with single mothers and fatherless homes. 80% of black children live in single-mother households. I don't care how well we can take care of our children by ourselves; **FATHERLESS HOMES ARE NOT GOD'S WILL FOR US AND OUR CHILDREN.** And yes, I am aware of death and divorces, etc. I can overlook those numbers. But most are single mothers, with multiple children from different fathers.

Ladies say it with me loud and unashamed; **MARRIAGE IS A GOAL!!**

Do You Have Boyfriend Insanity?

What is the boyfriend's insanity? It is doing the same thing with multiple boyfriends while expecting a different result. Many little girls in our culture are taught and trained to have boyfriends from an early age. Think about it; you had your first boyfriend at what age? That boyfriend did not work out, so you broke up and got another boyfriend.

However, some get pregnant by their boyfriends as teenagers and become teen moms, as I did. And for most teen moms, the insanity begins and continues. They get another boyfriend, and when that does not work out, the boyfriend's insanity continues.

Many of these women attend college, and the boyfriend's insanity continues. And multiple boyfriends run through their girlfriends while in college, and the boyfriend's insanity continues. Many of these girlfriends graduate and wait for their college boyfriends to marry them.

However, many of these boyfriends move along to other girlfriends, leaving their old girlfriends behind. The next thing you know, you are 40 with six kids by multiple boyfriends, aka baby daddies.

In the meantime, many of these women are still single. But they still want to get married and waiting for a good man to come in and clean up all your baggage. Yet, you have had several boyfriends throughout your life who have not married you. Remember, my now-husband was never my boyfriend.

On my husband and I seventh wedding anniversary, I asked him why he married me. Guess what he asked me? He asked me why I married him and not that other guy. Did I tell you that I dated and was open to dating other guys up to three months before my husband proposed? Lol

I sure did; I stopped dating other guys when he laid out his plan for marriage for me, his income, how he could provide a comfortable life for us. And yes, we started looking at rings. Until then, I was open, willing, and able to date other guys.

But do you remember what dating is? Yes. Dating is gathering data so that you can make an informed decision. Dating is also the process of elimination. Now, ladies, I never told my #1 prospect that I was dating other guys. But I guess he assumed I was dating other guys because when he asked me about being exclusive, I told him I did not do boyfriends or believe in exclusivity.

Also, I was not available every time he called, texted, or wanted to go out. Often when my now-husband wanted to go out, I told him that I was busy or had other plans. Ladies, you need to learn to be unavailable and find something else to do other than sitting at home waiting for the guy you are dating to call and take you out.

Sssshhhhh, don't tell him, but many of those times, I was home, keeping myself busy and being unavailable to him. If he wanted to have all my time, he needed to make his intentions known and begin to live it out by putting a ring on my finger. Ladies, please stop being so available to every man that you date.

Find something else to do so you are not sitting at home looking at the phone, stalking his social media to see what he is doing. I bet if you get busy with your life and dating other guys, you will not have time to be a stalker. Stop the boyfriend's insanity, please!

How to Know If You Have Baby Daddy Insanity

Baby daddy insanity is popping babies out with every man you lay down with while wanting a husband. Some women had a baby as a teen or young adult. That situationship did not work out, so you got with another guy, and boom, you had another kid. Then that baby daddy situationship did not work out, so you get with another guy, and here comes another baby.

Now you are up to three babies and, often, three baby daddies. The crazy thing about many women that I talk with is that they want to get married. So, even though these women want to be married, they continue to pop babies out with every man they lay down with, hoping that one will marry them. Please note that I have a biblical perspective on sex and babies. Do we mess up at times? Yes!

In the meantime, these women are not thinking about the effects all these various men would have on their children. And because there are often multiple fathers, the kids are treated differently. Additionally, there are emotional and psychological factors that many mothers do not think about when it comes to their children.

Remember, I was a teen mom at age sixteen. So please don't have an attitude about my above statement. For us to make changes, we need to know and accept the truth. If my father in the faith did not pull me to the side and talk to me, I would have probably ended up in the baby daddy insanity. But when I was 17 years old, my father told me that I should not have any more kids out of wedlock if I wanted to get a good husband.

My father also said that a divorced woman with five kids is valued more than a woman who has never been married with five kids from various fathers. And even though my mentality was not to be a baby mama, if I did not take charge of my future, I probably would have been caught up in the baby daddy insanity.

So, I decided that I would save myself for marriage and not have any more babies out of wedlock. My father also told me that neither should I place myself in a position to make another decision if I would have gotten pregnant.

Thankfully, I got married at 35, my daughter was 19, and at the publication of this book, my wonderful husband and I just celebrated our seventh wedding anniversary. Interestingly, I asked my husband if he would have married me if I had multiple children, and he was nice about it, but he would not have.

See, ladies, men of value will overlook one baby as a teen because we did not know any better. But multiple kids for multiple men outside of the covenant of marriage says a lot about us. It says we don't value ourselves; we don't love ourselves and the kids we continue to have in the cycle of insanity.

It also says that we don't think about our future and all these children we continue to have, as many kids are born in poverty. Men of value and substance think about the future, legacy, and life they can afford their children.

Also, men of value think about an inheritance for their children. So, my single mommies that want to get married, today is the day for you to make up your mind to NOT have any more kids with men who have not married you.

Additionally, think about it; some women have the attitude of having all these kids with no baby daddy contributing but expect their new husbands to foot the bill for these kids. Then get mad at the men that do not want them and their kids as if he SHOULD take them and their children.

My question is, where are the baby daddies? Where are those men you laid down with and created those precious little lives with? Now, I am not saying women with kids cannot get a good husband, but I am saying we need to be mindful! Can we stop getting angry at men who don't want to take responsibility for our children that are not theirs?

I am grateful every day that the Lord blessed me with my Boaz, who accepted and loved my daughter as his own. I am and will forever be grateful. However, if I had more than one child, I know that my husband would not have married me. So, ladies, please stop having all these children out of the marriage covenant with dusties and bums when you want to be married.

Your Boyfriend Might Be Keeping You Single

Ladies let's face it; many of you are not married because your boyfriends are keeping you away from your husbands. Your boyfriend is keeping you single. How? Because you are sitting there waiting for your boyfriend of twenty eleven years to marry you. All at the same time, wondering why he has not married you yet.

You see, some of you met a man, fell in love with him, set your eyes on him as if he was the prize, popped babies out, and then demanded that he married you. Even after you have wasted years waiting for him to marry you, you sat there and hoped. And all this time, you are wondering why he has not married you yet!

Well, it's because he is not your husband. You played the fool thinking that if you would sex him to a proposal, have his babies, wash, cook, clean, and prove yourself to be wifey material, then surely, he would eventually marry you. Ladies, your boyfriend might very well be keeping you single by keeping you away from your husband. Your husband, aka BOAZ, is looking for you, but he can't find you because you're up underneath BOZO, the fool.

Here's a question for you. When will you stop being a foolish woman and get some sense and realize that your boyfriend and or baby daddy is not going to marry you? And that is just using you to get ready for the next woman-his wife?

Why Is It So Hard to Say Goodbye?

How many stories have you heard of women getting their hearts broken by their boyfriends? In my opinion, it's crazy for women to continue to give their hearts to boyfriend after boyfriend. It begs the question when they eventually meet their husbands, will they have any heart left? Why is it so hard for women to walk away from men who have mistreated, used, and abused them?

Soul Ties

There are several reasons why some women stay with men wasting years of their lives, waiting for them to marry them. However, there is one critical factor we hardly ever talk about. And that's the topic of soul ties. Soul ties, what's that? To understand what soul ties are, let's define man's makeup, aka human. Like God, man is a tri-part being. The Godhead consists of God the Father, God the Son, and God the Holy Spirit. God is one with three different characteristics.

Likewise, humans or man consists of three parts also. The makeup of man consists of spirit, soul, and body. The first part of the tripart man is our spirit, man. Our spirit is the part of us that is most like God. Remember when God was telling Adam about The Tree of Knowledge of Good and Evil in the Garden of Eden in Genesis 2:17? What did God tell Adam about the Tree of Good and Evil?

God told Adam that he could eat of every tree in the garden except The Tree of Knowledge of Good and Evil. God told Adam that he would surely die if he ate from The Tree of Good and Evil. Well, Adam disobeyed God, and he and Eve ate from The Tree of the Knowledge of Good and Evil. However, it took Adam almost a thousand years to physically die. Apparently, God was talking about another type of death. God was talking about Adam dying spiritually.

So, when Adam ate from the tree, his spirit man died in the Garden of Eden. The second part of humans is our soul, which is also three parts. Our soul consists of our will, intellect, and emotions. All three parts of our souls present us with different issues and challenges we need to deal with. But the most essential part of our souls, in my opinion, is our·emotions. I believe we have most of our issues, trials, tribulations, and tests in our emotions.

And finally, the third and final makeup of humans is our bodies, also known as our earth suit. Our bodies are our rights or authority to operate in the earth realm. So human or man is a spirit, possesses a soul, and lives in a body. Therefore, soul ties are formed when your soul (spirit, soul, and body) is tied, entangled, and webbed together with another person's soul.

God's initial intention was for us only to have healthy soul ties with our husbands or mates. And of course, our families. I don't know about you, but I have had unhealthy soul ties with men that were not my husband. And it took years of changing my thinking, praying, reading my Bible to renew my mind and seek the face of the Lord.

Additionally, I fasted a lot and laid in the presence of the Lord to get my soul untied from those men so that I could have a healthy soul tie with my husband. Look back over your own life and dating portfolio. How many breakups and heartbreaks have you had? How long did it take for you to get over each man you broke up with? How many men are your souls still tied to that you have yet to get untied from? Will you be able to have a healthy marriage with your husband?

How to Stop Being a Girlfriend

Surprisingly, many women who settle for girlfriend status and shacking up are Church Girls. Look around your churches; many are filled with the kids of single moms. Now, now, I know some will be quick to say those single moms didn't make those kids alone. While true, how many of you ladies can agree that it's time for us to take control of our ability to procreate?

I was recently shocked to learn that 80% of black children live in single mothers' homes. I also learned that 70% of black women are chronically single or will never get married. I find it shocking that there is such an alarming number of children of color in a single mother's home.

If most black women are not getting married, where are all these children coming from? Fortunately, though the number of children of color living below the poverty limit has fallen, many still live in poverty. So, ladies, how many of you know that it's time for us to stop procreating with bums, deadbeats, and men who don't want to be our husbands and fathers of our children.

Ladies, please do not think of this as me "judging" but an observation so that we can stop the generational curses. And yes, many men in the church and, yes, even the pastor and deacons, have fathered some of these fatherless children. So, you see, ladies, we need to keep our legs closed to everyone while single. Because, like the old folks used to say "mama"s baby, but papa's maybe."

More children are being born to unwed parents in many churches than there are married couples. So, if you didn't know, let me tell you, "SAVED, SINGLE WOMEN ARE HAVING SEX AND

BABIES!" So, saved girls, it's time for us to get back to the basics, and as I wrote in my book '*The Naked Wife*,' TAKE THE COOKIE OFF THE TABLE!

Begin here:

1. Love yourself, your body, and your eggs.
2. Honor your body and present it to God as a living sacrifice.
3. Renew your mind about what God says about marriage.
4. Learn your identity in Christ; read my book "*In Christ I Am.*"
5. Know your worth and stop putting yourself on clearance.
6. Plan out your dating journey. Read my book "*23 Types of Guys You Might Meet.*"
7. Activate your dating plan.
8. Date accordingly and for marriage only.

How to Renew Your Mind from Girlfriend to Wife Mentality

Renewing your mind from girlfriend to wife mentality will take work, sacrifice, and diligence. Here are a few steps you can take to begin your wife mentality journey:

1. Make up your mind that you will not have any or any more children outside of the bonds and covenant of marriage. Additionally, my father, in the faith, warned me that neither should I place myself in the position to make another decision if I got pregnant. In other words, ladies, TAKE THE COOKIES OFF THE TABLE!
2. Educate yourself on what dating is and how-to date. You can read my book; *23 Types of Guys You Might Meet.*
3. Date with a Purpose: Why are you dating? Is it for sex, money, or the covenant of marriage?
4. Know what you want in a husband: do you know what you want in a husband? Can you say seven things you want in a husband and how those things will better your life and marriage?
5. What type of husband do you want? Do you want a provider husband, a 50/50, or an 80/20 husband? A fixer-upper, build a male, hobo-sexual, or someone who needs you to provide for him?
6. Do you know what type of men you like? Businessmen, blue-collar, average, athletes, etc.
7. Environment: When you know the type of men you like, find out where they are and place yourself in their environment.

Reminder: Ladies, please remember that it is critical that the husband you choose is a man that you can honor, respect, admire, look up to and who can be an example to you and your children.

Why You Should Date for Marriage ONLY

Many women waste years waiting for ONE man to marry them because they do not understand the basic concept of dating. You can read more extensively about what dating is in my book *23 Types of Guys You Might Meet.*

What is dating? Dating is skillfully gathering data so that you can make an informed decision about the men you are dating. Dating is also the process of elimination. In other words, ladies do not allow a man to waste years of your life waiting for him to marry you. Only to find out after five babies that he does not want to marry you. Besides, when most men say they do not want to get married, the *"to you"* part is silent.

Most men will lay up and have babies with you with no intention of marrying you. In the meantime, you are giving them all the sex they want. Additionally, you wash, cook, and clean, work ten jobs to "help" them. Also, you give them your best years while you wait for them to get ready to marry you. Only for them to get up and do what they said they did not want to do and marry another woman. Unfortunately, most men will use you as bed warmers until they find their ONE.

So, ladies, if you want to get married, sit your hips down and learn how to gather data on the men you meet and date. Know what you want in a husband so that when you meet and talk to a guy, you can decide if you're going to continue to gather data on him. Would you believe that most of the men I dated, I did not go out with them? Why? Because by talking to them, I knew I did not want to waste my time.

And remember, what is dating? Dating is gathering data so that you can make an informed decision. How? For example, number one on my list was a man that was born again. So, if I met a man who was not born again, guess what? No need for us to continue getting to know each other. Now, many foolish and desperate women, aka pick-meshas, would say, well, you can get him saved. That is a huge mistake many Christian women make. Many Christian women marry unsaved men, and their lives and marriages are a living hell.

Another example is number four on my list of what I wanted in a husband who has a good job (career) and can provide for my daughter and me. So, if I met a man who was in-between jobs, couldn't keep a job, and hadn't worked in years, guess what, ladies? There was no need to continue with him. I would drop him and move along. No hard feelings, emotions, and no pity for him. Goodbye!

Why? I wanted a man who has a good job and could provide. Many foolish women, aka pickmeshas, would say, oh, you could fix him up and fill out job applications for him and help him find a job. Unfortunately, what those foolish women, aka pickmeshas, don't understand is that they will have to stay on this man to find a job and keep it for the rest of the relationship and marriage.

Why? Because he is not self-motivated, he didn't have a vision for his life. And a man with no vision will perish. And any woman who attaches herself to a visionless man is foolish. And she, along with their children, will struggle and often suffer too.

Instead, ladies, choose a man who has a job (career) that he loves, who can provide a comfortable life for you. Additionally, let's think about providing. If he does not have a job to provide for himself, how can he provide for you? Just maybe he is looking for a woman who can provide for him? Here again, many foolish women would say, "Oh,

I make enough for us." These same foolish women marry these men and are ok with being breadwinners.

However, a short time after, these same women who signed up to provide for their men get tired of being the providers. Why? Because God did not create us to be providers. These women want to change their roles, not understanding that they already set the tone for their marriages.

Ladies, please stop wasting your time, date accordingly, and choose good men. As for men who have a fixed monthly income, please think things through wisely, ladies. Your life, marriage, and future of your children will only go as far as the vision of your husband.

Do You know That a Husband IS a Choice?

Again, dating is gathering data about men so that you can make an informed decision about them. Additionally, dating is a process of elimination. So, if dating is about gathering data to make an informed decision, then, obviously, a husband is a choice, right? While God might reveal to a few sisters who their husbands are, most of us must make ourselves available to be found. And men need to get out there and find their good thing.

Now, if a husband is a choice, who do you choose from? Yes, my dears, you get to choose your husband. To some women, the statement *a husband is a choice* means finding a man and making him marry you. No, ladies, that is not what that means.

Proverbs 18:22 says, «**He who finds a wife finds a good thing and obtains favor from the Lord**." One of the verses my father in the faith asked me to commit to memory. My dad would say if ten men found me, I must choose one of them. What does 'find' mean? Men who have prepared themselves to be husbands will be looking for a wife. He needs to search for her, pursue her, and overtake her with his offer of marriage.

But hold on to your stilettos, ladies. You have rights when it comes to marriage. My dad would say, "Janice, he finds you, but you choose him." So, **Psalm 65:4: "Blessed is the man You choose and cause to approach You, that he may dwell in Your courts. We shall be satisfied with the goodness of Your house, Of Your holy temple."**

So, the men find us, but we get to choose them. Every man looking for a wife is not looking for one to profess his love to provide for and protect. Some men are looking for a woman who can take care of them.

Therefore, ladies, you need to date and gather data on the men who pursue you. Vet or screen them carefully. You must weed through all those men and choose the best man who wants to marry you and be your husband.

What Do You Want a Husband?

Do you know what you want in a husband? Have you ever thought about what kind of man you want to spend the rest of your life with? I submit to you that most women do not know what they want in a husband? Why? Because if you did, you would not waste years of your lives waiting for men who told you they do not want to get married or is not ready to get married, to marry you.

When I was single, I always knew what I wanted in my husband. I wrote down everything I could think of. And the more I dated, the more I refined my husband list. My husband's list would result in me doing a husband test on the guys I dated. The husband test was seeing if the guys I dated matched my list.

Sadly, the church has taught for years that we don't need a list when believing God for our husbands. Yet, the divorce rate is worst in the church than in the world. Contrary to how some think in the church, there is nothing wrong with having a list of what you want in a husband. This way, each man that approaches you will have to pass your husband's test to continue to date you.

Remember that you can read more in my book *23 Types of Guys You Might Meet* about dating. Again, dating is collecting data about the men you are meeting to make an informed decision about them. Dating is also the process of elimination. You are to gather information about various guys and decide about them based on what you want in a husband.

So, when some of the guys you date and gather information on do not match up to your husband list and don't pass your husband test, you need to drop them like a hot potato and move along. Let me warn you that the husband test takes discipline. And it requires you not to get emotional and become attached to the men you date.

The husband test also requires you to be disciplined, rooted, and grounded in what you desire in a husband. Additionally, diligence and discernment are essential. More importantly, never fall in love! And for goodness's sake, please do not have sex with the men you date.

Remember, dating is for gathering data ONLY! Dating is not for sex, shacking up, having babies, or splitting bills. Avoiding sex with the men you date will prevent babies out of wedlock and sexually transmitted diseases. Also, soul ties, and unrealistic expectations from men who have not gone through the process to profess their love, provide for and protect you.

But most importantly, as women of faith, we are committed to doing things God's way. Obeying God's word will give us a harvest of blessings. And please do not mention safe sex. Because for the born-again believer, the only safe sex is SAVED SEX. God's only approval of sex is in the covenant of marriage. Have most of us fall in the area of sex? Yes!

However, when we know better, we do better. And I would imagine after so many heartbreaks, disappointments, and wasted time, you would want to do things God's way. God's only approval of how we are to live and conduct our lives is HIS WAYS!!

How to Make a Husband List

As mentioned before, the husband test requires you to decide if the men you date is what you want in a husband. However, many women do not seem to think about one crucial factor. And that's if you are what the men want. In other words, do your common core goals align. If the men you are dating are not what you desire in a husband, you must drop them and move on to other men. Remember, though, that dating is ONLY about DATA.

Therefore, you should not meet one man and hang up your dating stilettos because you think he is the one. NO WASTED TIME LADIES! It took me years to develop my husband's list that I have now. The more I dated, the more I refined my husband list, learned about myself, and discovered what I wanted and liked in my husband.

I cannot tell you the pushback I get from church folks about a husband list. I just smile because most of those who want to challenge me have been divorced three times or have never been married. I know a ton of women sitting in churches, waiting for God to bring their husbands to them to say, "This is your husband." Many of those women are in their fifties, sixties, and seventies, still waiting on God.

Here's a quick sample of my husband's list below. While it is not an exhaustive list, I want to give you an example so that you can begin to make your husband's list if you do not have one. My husband's list consisted of ten variables, including negotiables and non-negotiables. I never compromise on my non-negotiables, but I was open to negotiating on my negotiables.

Why do I need both negotiable and non-negotiables? Because no one is perfect, and our mates will not be perfect, though still perfect for us. We all must make concessions when it comes to our mates.

It is essential that the concessions we make, we can live with them and not regret them later. A concession is not about settling. Please note that I might use the word compromise interchangeably with concession.

Here is a short sample of my husband's list. I will be writing a book soon on the husband's list.

My husband had to be:

1. **Born again:** I was only interested in men who were born again. So, if I met a man who was everything else, but he was not born again, guess what I did? I would drop him and move on. Many women would try to get him saved. Not me!

2. **A Tither**: I am a tither and wanted a husband who was also a tither. I believe tithing is personal, reflecting our faith in Jesus Christ. So, if I met a man who had everything else but was not a tither, I would drop him and move on. I know many women who try to convince men to be tithers. The result is a struggling marriage and never-ending fights about money.

3. **A Gentleman**: I love a masculine man and a gentleman, which can only be taught to a boy by another man. If I met a man who had everything else but was not a gentleman, I would drop him and move on. And ladies, please forget this foolishness about teaching a male how to be a man. As a woman, you've never been a man, so how can you teach a male how to be a man?

4. **Has a Good Career**: The man I wanted was one with a good and established career. I did not want a man in between jobs, cannot get a job, can't keep a job or anything like that. So, if I met a man who

had everything else but didn't have a good job that would enable him to provide a good and comfortable life for my daughter and me, I would drop him and move on.

This man with a good job had to be one who will provide for us independent of me. In other words, he would not need my income to pay bills. And for me, I do not do 50/50! I would not marry a man who needed me to help him provide for me.

I often get pushbacks from many women because they feel that if a man is not where he needs to be, they should help him get there. I do not believe I should have to help a man get to the place he needs to be to be a husband to me. The only male that I am to help to become a man is my son.

I do not believe I should have to help a grown man who wants to marry me to become a man. The man who would be my husband was a man who prepared himself to profess his love, provide, and protect me. Therefore, I was only interested in men who prepared themselves to be husbands because, after all, I was a wife.

Yes, there have been many women who have helped unprepared males to become their husbands. Sadly, many of those men often leave their mom-wives to find other women who will appreciate them for the men those mom-wives build them to be. Remember, a husband is a choice, so why not just choose an already built man?

Think of the story of Adam and Eve. God made Adam, placed him in the garden, and gave him a vision. Adam established his vision and built up his business. God then said, "It is not good for man to be alone." And so, God brought Adam his wife, Eve. Eve only had to sit back and enjoy Adam's vision and hard work.

On the other hand, Adam was to show off all that he has done to Eve. Adam was to boast about everything he had accomplished. So, ladies, when you have your husband's list down, you date accordingly to see if the men pass your husband's test. As you talk to the men you date, you gather your data based on your list. And if they don't measure up for you, you drop them and move on.

As you date, aka gather data on the men you date, you should not have any emotional attachments to them. Speak wisely, keep your eyes open, pay attention to everything they say and do. Keep your legs and mouth closed, hands clasped, and do not stay on the phone for hours with them. Limit contact and keep busy by dating several guys at once and be unavailable sometimes. Ladies, you must learn to date, aka gather data without committing to the men you date.

Additionally, there are three Ps of a good and godly husband. And you can read more in my other book, *23 Types of Guys You Might Meet*, but I will mention them here briefly. Firstly, a good and godly husband should be able to: Profess his love for his wife. Secondly, a good and godly husband should be able to protect his wife. And, thirdly, a good and godly husband should be able to provide a comfortable life for his wife.

Ladies, if the man you want to marry is not able to do all three of the P's, please tell me why would you marry him? Why would you turn your life over to him? Why would you submit to a man who cannot profess his love, provide for you, and protect you?

How to Accept or Decline Dates?

When I met my husband, it took him a month to call me to schedule a date. When he finally called, I talked to him for only a few minutes, enough time for him to plan a date. You see, my father always told me that if a man wants me, he will do the work and pursue me. When Michael finally called, he wanted to take me out that evening for drinks, but I declined.

Then he asked about taking me out the next day, and once again, I declined. I told him no, that I had a date and would not be available. Michael then proceeded to ask if he could take me out on Saturday, and I told him no; I had plans. Yet again, he asked if he could take me out for brunch on Sunday after church, and I told him no, I was busy and already had plans. He went on to ask about taking me out for dinner on Monday, and I agreed.

Once we agreed on the day, I was available, Michael said he would make reservations at one of the most upscale restaurants that sat by the river with New York's skyline. When I asked him where it was located, he stated that it was about an hour away with traffic. I told him no, that it was too far for me to be away from my daughter, Alexia. Because in the event of an emergency, I would need to get to Lexi immediately.

So, my now Mr. Wonderful asked me to choose a comfortable restaurant for me. I told him Applebee's, which was five minutes from my house. His response was, "APPLEBEE'S!??" Lol. He could not believe I wanted to go to Applebee's. We still laugh about that almost eight years of marriage later—more on this in another book, coming soon.

Monday, the evening of the date, Michael called to cancel because he was stuck in a meeting and asked if we could reschedule. I told him that I would need to check my schedule to see when I was available. But later, Michael called me back and said to me that he called a car service to pick him up to meet me for dinner because he wanted to see me. He worked in New York on Wall Street, and I lived in New Jersey.

Michael offered to pick me up, but I declined. Why? Because he is a stranger, and I do not trust strangers. STRANGER DANGER. A few hours later, we met at Applebee's. It was raining and cold, so I wore a pair of skinny jeans and a beige turtleneck with some beige boots. Michael got to the restaurant before me and had a beautiful bouquet for me.

Oh, he was so handsome. He had a gold business shirt with black tie and black slacks. I remember it like it was yesterday. Lol! Before our entrée came, he asked to take me out again the next day, which was Tuesday. Guess what I said? I declined his request for a date and told him I was busy. Then he asked if he could take me out on Wednesday, and I accepted.

During our date on Wednesday, he asked if he could take me out again on Thursday, and I declined. He then asked about taking me out on Friday, and I accepted. During our Friday night date, he asked if he could take me out for breakfast on Saturday morning because he had to travel on Sunday. I accepted since he would be traveling for about a week. For Saturday, I asked him if he would like to go for a walk before breakfast, and he agreed.

You see, ladies, I was picking up that he was interested in me, so I wanted to do some more intense research on him. I ran track when I was younger, and he was twelve years my senior, so I wanted to see if he could keep up with me. So, we talked as we walked on the track. Usually, it takes about an hour to walk around, but we walked it in about 45 minutes.

Sunday, Michael called early to tell me that his car service was picking him up, and he was going to stop by his church to drop off his tithes and offering. But before he goes to the airport, he said he would like to come and give me a hug. Hallelujah, a man who tithes was my number two on my list of things I wanted in a husband! Ladies, can you say my ears perked up? When he stopped by, of course, he came with flowers.

Some foolish women and pickmeshas have criticized me for letting him wait to take me out. They asked what if he had changed his mind. My response was, "Ok, if he changed his mind." What was I missing after he waited to make contact for a whole month? I had not heard from him in a month, but I was still going out on dates with other guys? I was busy dating. Why should I stop my life to accommodate him on such short notice?

See, ladies, when you keep busy dating other guys, you don't have time to worry about one guy who didn't take you out. And if you stay active, you won't have to jump at a first date offer. Granted, I was not busy dating that weekend, but he didn't need to know that.

For all he knew, I could not go out with him when he called because I had a date!! And ladies, I kept this same posture throughout the whole time we were dating. It was only three months before he proposed; I stopped dating other guys when we started ring shopping.

The #1 Mind-Blowing Reason You Continue to Attract the Wrong Guys

Many women seek my advice about why they only attract boyfriends, fixer-uppers, hobosexuals, and men who need healing. Hobosexuals are males who get with women for a place to live. Ladies, we attract the type of men we do because there is something on us. If you have a girlfriend spirit, then you will attract a boyfriend.

You attract hobosexuals because you advertise yourself as someone who men can come and live with. And that you are open to taking care of men. Masculine women attract feminine men who need their women to defend them. Women who want to heal men and fix them up will attract broken men. So, ladies, if you continue to attract the same type of broken men and not a man you want, then look in the mirror.

You might just be attracting the men you do because you're giving off the wrong spirit. However, if you have a wife's spirit, you will attract a husband. **Proverbs 18:22** says, "He who finds a wife finds a good thing, **And obtains favor from the Lord.**" Notice the verse did not say he who finds a girlfriend finds a good thing. So, women who walk in the spirit of a wife, knowing that they will accept nothing less than a prepared husband, will attract husband material.

Wives are not wishy-washy. Today, you want to be a wife, but tomorrow, you will accept being a girlfriend. The Bible talks about a double-minded person being unstable in all their ways. Make up in your mind that you are a wife, and you will accept nothing less than a man who wants to marry you. And yes, I know it's hard out there.

One of the prayers I prayed when I was single was for God to hide me from men who were not husband material. And for a long time, I didn't get asked out on dates. Neither was I meeting guys I would go out for dinner with. As mentioned before, I used that time to get rooted and grounded in the Lord. I also perfected my husband list to know what I wanted in a husband.

Now, ladies, you know that the enemy is a counterfeit, so he will always send counterfeits to test you. For example, before I met my husband, the enemy sent a counterfeit that looked like my husband. However, because I spent time establishing myself in being rooted and grounded in what I wanted, I shook him off and did not settle.

And a short time after, I met my wonderful husband. Now, ladies, I had to run like Joseph, the 11th son of Jacob, and Rachel's first son. But I'm so glad I did. That man was hot on my heels. Lol!!

The important thing was, I knew he was not my husband but was a counterfeit instead.

You cannot settle for less than. If you meet a man and know that he is not husband material, please do not try to make him your husband. And there are several other reasons why women continue to attract the wrong guys, but this is the one I wanted to mention.

1 Shocking Reason Why You Are Not Meeting High-Quality Men

For years I did not meet any men I would go out for dinner with, let alone marry. At age 28, I decided that I would no longer go out with guys just to go out. I had gotten so good at knowing what I wanted in a husband that I could tell within the first minute or two of talking to a guy if I wanted to go out with him.

I hated wasting time, so I saved time going out with guys by knowing what I wanted and having my list committed to memory and heart. I know many dating coaches suggest going out with every man, regardless of if you think there is something there or not. Today, I am against that because I wasted time doing that in my early 20s.

For example, if I met a man who was not born again, why should I waste time going out with him? I can hear a million reasons now like: you could lead him to the Lord, he could be a friend, etc. Nope!! I did not need another male friend; I needed a husband!

And if I met men who were not born again, and they used the "but you can lead me to Jesus" bait, my father in the faith told me to give them his number. They could call him, and he would happily lead them to the Lord. Lol!! Instead of wasting time with men that I knew were not suitable for me, I used that time to study, learn more about dating, and work on my first book, *Praying for Our Children.*

Once I completed my first book, I was on my bed one evening after celebrating my 34th birthday, and suddenly, I got a revelation. I was 34 and still single! Right then, The Holy Spirit spoke to me to get up, get dressed, and go out. I jumped up, grabbed my computer, and searched for events. I found a networking event for businesspeople and decided to attend. After all, I was a new author, so this would be an excellent opportunity to market my book.

When I was writing *23 Types of Men You Might Meet*, I realized that it took me forever to meet my husband because I was not strategically placing myself in the environment where the type of man I liked was. For years I sat in my little family churches believing that God would send my husband to find me there.

Little did I understand that the type of men I liked did not attend those little family churches; the men I wanted were sitting under pastors like them. My husband's pastor is a lawyer and his frat brother. My husband is an executive who works on Wall Street, and those types did not attend little churches like mine.

I liked and wanted to marry the type of man of means, high quality, and high value. My husband's type of men surrounds themselves with men who are like them. They are in a space all by themselves. They don't hang out at the neighborhood corner church.

As **Proverbs 27:17; Iron sharpeneth iron; so a man sharpeneth the countenance of his friend.** So, ladies, is it possible to have not met your Mr. Wonderful because you are not strategically placing yourself in the right environment?

Why You Might Not Have Met Your Husband Yet

As mentioned earlier, I have always wanted to get married. I made sure to serve in the church, as serving is our first responsibility in the Kingdom of our Lord and Savior Jesus Christ. At nineteen years old, I preached my first sermon, and I taught Sunday school and Bible studies until my early thirties.

During that time, I always thought that I would have met my husband while serving in the church. To my surprise, I was in my early thirties, still not married, and with not one prospect insight. November 2010, I was going to the bank, and I was talking to the Lord about how I haven't met my husband yet.

The Holy Spirit said, "*lookup*." When I looked up, it was cloudy and looked as if it would rain. The Holy Spirit said, "*The reason you have not met your husband yet is because he is held up. Many women have laid claims to him as their husband, but he is not their husband. So, pray that he is released.*" Can you say "WOW"? I prayed right there and then.

And a year later, I met my husband on November 4th. Ladies, many of you are not married because you have laid claims to some men who do not want to marry you. Many of you have debased yourself from wife status to girlfriend, which has caused the husband's blessing and anointing to stop flowing in your life.

If you have been putting all your marital hopes and dreams in one man's flimsy, possibly full of holes basket, hoping that he will marry you, this might be your opportunity to walk away and pray for your husband to be released.

The same way you might be holding up another woman's husband, it might be the same way another woman is holding up your husband. As my father in the faith would always say, TURN HIM ALOSE!!

When you want to be married, you need to focus on renewing your mind about marriage. You need to know what you want in a husband without a doubt. You need to be available to date several guys at once. Additionally, you need to be open to strategically place yourself in the environment the type of men you like are.

So, you see, ladies, you don't have time waiting around for some man you've been shacking up with for years to marry you. Remember, contrary to the lies you were told; MARRIAGE IS A GOAL. And to accomplish your goals, you must work at them.

1 Revolutionary Truth You Might Not Want to Hear

Ladies, I know that you want to get married, but this is the time to take inventory of you and where you are. Some of you do not need another boyfriend or a husband. Some of you are so damaged, hurt, used up, and misused that you only need JESUS. You need to allow Jesus to heal you of all the pain and hurt so that you can be well enough to receive your husband and be his helpmate.

The following excerpt is taken from my book *23 Types of Guys You Might Meet.*

... I want to talk to you about a man named Jesus. If you already know him, praise the Lord. If you don't know the Lord in the pardon of your sins, allow me to introduce him to you. Jesus? Yes, the Lord Jesus Christ. One of my favorite stories in the Bible is from **John 4**, where Jesus was traveling with his disciples. The Bible declares, "Jesus NEEDED to go through Samaria."

However, Jesus instructed his disciples to go on ahead of him; he did not want to be distracted because they wouldn't understand what was about to happen. Shocked and dismayed by Jesus's request, the disciples nevertheless obeyed and went on ahead of him to buy food.

Jesus came to a well, and he was "tired." Then came a woman. She was not named but is known as the Woman at the Well. When I was a little girl in Sunday School, we used to sing a song that said, *"The woman of Samaria, the woman, she left her waterpot and gone." (Jamaican accent.)*

As the story progressed, Jesus asked her for some water. She asked Jesus why he was asking her for water. She was a Samaritan, you see, and Jews and Samaritans had no dealings with each other. The Samaritan was known "as a mixed breed" of people from when the Jews were in captivity. Then Jesus mentioned to her about the gift of life and asked if she knew who he was. More importantly, if she truly knew who he was, she would know to ask him for the living water.

The Woman at the Well responded that Jesus had nothing to draw with, the well was deep, and from where can he get this living water? She was a bit slow to get the revelation of who she was talking to and asked if he was more significant than her father, Jacob, who dug the well. Jesus responded that whoever drinks of this well will continue to be thirsty again, but whoever drinks from the living water will never be thirsty again. The living water will be a well springing up into everlasting life.

Immediately, her ears perked up, and she got interested and asked, "Sir, give me this water that I might never thirst again or come to draw water from the well."

"Go call your husband and come back," Jesus said.

"I don't have a husband," she said.

And Jesus responded, "you have well said because you have had five husbands." Finally, she got that Jesus was not just another man, but he was a prophet, the Messiah, the Christ.

After that, the disciples returned, and the Woman at the Well left her waterpot, ran to the city, and told everyone to come to see a man who had told her all about herself. And isn't he the Messiah?

Princesses, this woman was an outcast because she had five husbands, and I am sure she had done things with other women's husbands, also. When the women went to get water at the well, they would go early in the morning while it was cool or in the evening. However, this outcast woman went alone in the heat of the date.

Additionally, the women would go as a group for safety reasons. This woman was at the well in the middle of the day, alone and in the heat. Many scholars believe that she was ashamed to walk with the other women, but she was probably trying to get husband number six. But, praise Jesus, she met Jesus, the seventh and final man who could quench the unyielding thirst. Note that seven is the number of completion.

Here is a significant fact that I want to point out. Do you notice how Jesus told her to call her husband? Jesus wanted her to see and realize that she was broken, empty, and needed to be filled with his grace, mercy, and love.

Furthermore, another vital factor to keep in mind is that no one in the Bible who came to Jesus for healing remained sick or in the same place. Everyone who came to Jesus in need of healing made a change in their lives to follow him.

Therefore, my dear sister princesses, I want you to know that if you are broken, another man will not heal that pain, brokenness, and rejection. You see, many of us are seeking a man to fill a void when the only man who can is Christ Jesus. Only the Lord Jesus Christ can heal it.

You might have gone from man to man trying to get the living water from them, but the truth is the living water is only available through the Lord Jesus Christ. Like the Woman at the Well, please open your heart and your mouth and drink from Jesus Christ's living water.

Romans 10:9 says that if you will confess with your mouth the Lord Jesus Christ and believe in your heart that God raised him from the dead, you will be saved. Notice that it did not say confess your sins; instead, it said, confess Jesus Christ and believe in your heart that God raised him from the dead. Go ahead and do so right now in the name of Jesus Christ.

God bless you, and I am so excited for your new journey with the Lord Jesus Christ. Now, go in Christ, learn of him, and apply his word to your heart and life. Blessings always, and in due time, the Lord will manifest your husband as you continue to make yourselves available to be found. You can learn more about your new identity in Christ by reading my *In Christ I Am* series.

CONCLUSION

Nestled in the heart of the book of Genesis, beginning in the 29th chapter, is the introduction of the story of Jacob, Leah, and Rachel's tragic love triangle. This love triangle seems to shift the Jewish Nation's foundation and our Lord and Savior Jesus Christ's lineage. Additionally, Jacob, Leah, and Rachel's love triangle is a heartbreaking and tragic story for these two women who were also sisters.

However, Leah, Jacob, and Rachel's love triangle lay the foundation for the subtle delusionality (yes, I just made up a word. Lol) of some women who try to trap men into loving and marrying them by getting knocked up, aka pregnant. Many women try to entrap men who they love, but the men don't love them in return. The tragic love triangle of Leah, her younger sister Rachel and Jacob, the man they both loved, is a perfect example of trying to trap a man by having babies for him.

Though Moses, the author of Genesis, begins their story Genesis 29, Jacob's story started in Genesis 24 with Jacob's mother Rebekah and her older brother Laban. It is this same Laban, the Uncle of Jacob and father of both Leah and Rachel. I encourage you to read the entire passage in your free time. But I will give you a quick summary to help you understand the dysfunction between Leah, Jacob, and Rachel.

Laban, the older brother of Rebekah, Jacob's mother, helped her secure a good and wealthy husband in Isaac. Isaac is the beloved and promised son and only wealthy heir of the famous Abraham, the Jewish Nation's father. Rebekah, who became Isaac's wife, sadly was barren and could not get pregnant. Isaac prayed for Rebekah, and the Lord blessed her and opened her womb. The Lord blessed Rebekah and Isaac with twin boys Esau and Jacob.

While Rebekah was pregnant, the boys wrestled within her womb, and she prayed. The Lord told her that there were two nations in her womb and that the older son will serve the younger son. When Rebekah was giving birth, Esau, the older son, was coming out of the birth canal, he was red, and the nurse tied a red string on his hand to show that he was the firstborn. Because being the firstborn brings the inheritance and blessing of the father and the firstborn rights.

However, Jacob, the younger brother, grabbed Esau's heel and came out first. So, Jacob means heel-grabber, circumvent, supplant, trickster, deceiver and cheater. Rebekah loved Jacob more than his brother Esau who was a plain man. But Isaac loved Esau more because he was hairy and a hunter. The boys grew and became adults, and the differences between them were evident. The love of the parents for each boy was also noticeable.

As time would have it, it was time for Isaac to bestow the firstborn blessing upon Esau. So, Isaac told Esau to hunt for his famous venison and make him a meal. After Isaac ate, he would bestow the blessing upon Esau.

However, Rebekah, who overheard Isaac telling Esau about the blessing, constructed a plan with Jacob to deceive Isaac and steal the blessings from Esau. So, Rebekah cooked Isaac the meal just the way he liked it.

Then Rebekah took the best of Esau's clothes that she had in her tent and dressed Jacob in them. Rebekah then took the skin of baby goats and put them upon Jacob's hand and neck. Afterward, Rebekah sent Jacob with the meal to give to Isaac to get the blessing.

When Jacob brought the food to Isaac, Isaac suspected that something was off. So, he asked Jacob who he thought was Esau, how he returned so quickly. Jacob said the Lord your God brought it to him. Also, Isaac asked Jacob who he thought was Esau to come near him to feel him and see if it was his beloved son Esau.

When Jacob went to his father, Isaac felt his arm, and it was hairy. Isaac then said that the voice was that of Jacob, but he smelled and felt like Esau. And even though Isaac thought something was off, he went against his better judgment and blessed Jacob thinking it was Esau.

Sadly, when Esau returned with his meal, he was shocked to hear that someone already brought a meal to his father, Isaac. And that Isaac thought it was Esau, so he blessed him. That person was his younger brother Jacob who stole his blessing.

Poor Esau cried bloody murder and asked if there wasn't a blessing left for him. Isaac blessed Esau that his dwelling shall be the fatness of the earth and the dew of heaven. Then Esau threatened to kill Jacob as soon as their father Isaac dies. Esau also hated Jacob because of the blessing.

However, if you remember earlier in the story, God had already said that the older brother would serve the younger brother. Like many of us, Rebekah took it upon herself to try and help God out.

Additionally, there was a time when Esau came in from the field and was hungry. Well, his younger and domestic brother Jacob had cooked a delicious pot of stew. Esau begged Jacob to give him some of his stew. Jacob, who was always thinking about the blessing, bargain with Esau that he would give him some of his delicious stew if he would sell him his birthright.

Foolishly, Esau agreed to Jacob's offer and agreed to sell his birthright to Jacob for a pot of stew. It's apparent that Jacob's mind was always on the firstborn rights and blessing, while Esau didn't seem to care much about it. Therefore, Jacob thought day and night about the blessing and how to get it.

After Jacob stole his brother's Esau's blessing from their father, Isaac, Esau threatened to kill Jacob. However, word got back to Rebekah that Esau planned to kill Jacob. Rebekah called Jacob and told him that Esau planned to kill him. Rebekah instructed Jacob to flee to her brother Laban in Haran. Rebekah told Jacob that once Esau was no longer angry, she would send for him.

Rebekah then went to Isaac and told him that she was weary of her life and if Jacob took a wife of the Canaanites' daughters, what good her life would be. You see, Esau married many of the Canaanites' daughters to upset his mother, Rebekah. Rebekah, however, didn't want Jacob to marry any of the daughters of the heathens.

So, Isaac calls Jacob and told Jacob not to marry any of the Canaanites' daughters. Instead, Jacob should go to Padanaram, the house of Bethuel, his grandfather, and take a wife from her brother Laban's daughters. Isaac then affirmed the blessings upon Jacob and sent him away.

And when Esau saw that Isaac was displeased with the land's women, he went to Isaac's eldest and forgotten brother Ishmael and married his daughter. Marrying Ishmael's daughter was all done to spite his parents.

Jacob in Haran

As Jacob approached the land of Haran, he came to a well where shepherds were waiting for the sheep to gather so that they could give them water. He asked the men about Laban, the son of Nahor, and if he was well.

The men responded that Laban was well and that his daughter Rachel was coming to water her father's Laban's sheep. When Jacob saw Rachel, he rolled away the massive stone and watered Laban, his uncle's sheep. Jacob then kissed Rachel and cried and told her that he was Rebekah's son.

Rachel ran and told her father that Jacob, his sister's Rebekah son, had come. Laban then ran to meet Jacob, kissed, hugged him, and brought him to his house. Jacob told Laban everything that transpired and his purpose for coming to Haran.

So, Jacob stayed with Laban for about a month. After a month, Laban asked Jacob what his wages would be because he didn't want him to work for free. We then learn that Laban had two daughters. The eldest was Leah, and the younger was Rachel.

The Bible tells us more about the sisters; Leah was tender-eyed, but Rachel was beautiful and well-favored. Tender-eyed means weak, no sparkle, and not considered beautiful at that time. In other words, Leah had a lazy eye, was ugly and unattractive. However, Rachel was pretty and had a lovely figure.

Jacob responded to Laban's offer of naming his wages as Rachel's hand in marriage. Jacob stated that he would work seven years for Rachel, the younger daughter. The Bible tells us that those seven years seem like a few days because Jacob loved Rachel so much. At the end of the seven years, Jacob went to Laban and demanded that he gave him Rachel, his wife.

So, Laban gathered the men and planned a wedding for Jacob and Rachel to get married. On the night of the wedding feast, Laban took Jacob's new bride and brought her to Jacob. Jacob brought his wife to their wedding bed. All night, Jacob and his wife had a time of lovemaking and enjoyment.

The following day, Jacob awoke to discover that his new wife was not the beautiful and lovely-figured Rachel, the love of his life, but was instead the tender-eyed and unattractive Leah. Jacob ran and cried, screaming to Laban, asking him what he had done. Why did Laban trick him into marrying Leah?

Jacob protested that he only wanted one wife, his only true love, Rachel. Laban responded that it should not be done in their country that the younger sister should get married before the eldest one. Now, if you'll remember when Jacob was negotiating with Laban, Laban immediately accepted Jacob's offer. I think Laban had been plotting how to marry off his ugly daughter Leah all along. Instead of finding her a proper husband.

Jacob still loved and wanted to marry Rachel. So, Laban negotiated with Jacob again to work an additional seven years for Rachel, and he could also have her. However, Laban said Jacob could marry Rachel in 2 weeks after Leah's wedding feast was over. Two weeks later, Jacob married Rachel, and he loved her very much.

The Bible states that God noticed that Jacob didn't love Leah, so he opened her womb and blessed her with children. But the Lord shut up Rachel's womb, and she was not able to conceive. I have always thought God shutting up Rachel's womb was so unfair to both Jacob and Rachel.

Anyways, Leah got pregnant and had a son, who she named Reuben. Leah said the Lord has looked upon her affliction, and now her husband will love her. Sadly, for Leah, Jacob still didn't love her. Again, Leah conceived and had a son named Simon because the Lord heard that she was hated and had given her this son. Once again, Leah thought Jacob would love her because she has birthed him two sons. However, once again, Jacob still didn't love her.

Once more, Leah got pregnant and had a third son, whom she named Levi. Leah said this time Jacob would love her and join unto her because she had three sons for him. But even after three sons and Jacob seed being solidify, he still didn't love Leah.

Leah kept lying to herself while giving the pretty kitty to Jacob every time he came knocking. And for the fourth time, Leah got pregnant and had another son named Judah. But this time, a shift took place in Leah's heart, mind, soul, and spirit. Instead of hoping for Jacob to love her, Leah said, **"I WILL PRAISE THE LORD, THEREFORE!"** Then Leah stopped having children.

The Leah In Me

How many of you ladies can identify with poor Sister Leah? How many of you have wasted years of your life waiting, hoping, and praying that the man you love would love you back?

How many babies have you popped out for various men, thinking that they will love and marry you because of your babies? How many men have you tried to trap by getting pregnant, hoping that the baby will make them love and marry you?

How many meals have you cooked, and houses have you cleaned? How many walls have you climbed calling Jesus? Hoping that this time, the man you love would love you. When will you stop trying to trap a man into loving and marrying you? Who said you could have my kid, but you can't be M.R.S?

Poor Leah would sleep with Jacob every time he came knocking. And every time he laid with her, she would conceive and gave him the most precious thing a man could get- a son. Yet Jacob did not love Leah. Leah did everything she possibly could to get Jacob to notice her and love her.

The only thing Leah was good for to Jacob was her pretty kitty, her womb, and her ability to push sons out. Finally, one day after four sons, it occurred to Leah that she needed to stop trying to make Jacob love her and thank God for what she had.

Leah decided to give God praise for her children though this realization was temporary. But for a moment, Leah came to her senses and realized her worth. Leah realized that she needed to find solace in God, give Him praise, and stop forcing Jacob to love her.

Who Are You?

My dearest sister reading *10 Years a Girlfriend.* If you identify with Leah's story or any of the ladies I mentioned, I want to tell you who you are. You are not just a pretty kitty, a womb, and eggs for men to procreate with.

Sadly, I must tell you that you allowed men to use your body, mistreat you, and waste your time because you did not love yourself. But after reading *10 Years a Girlfriend,* I am sure you have realized that loving yourself is an absolute must.

And that you know that you need to love yourself, allow me to tell you who you are. You are not a toilet for men to release themselves in. You are not just your fried chicken, mac and cheese, and collard greens. You are not only a housekeeper who cleans and keeps your boyfriend's house. You are not a friend with benefits.

You are, however, a daughter of the King of Kings. You are so precious to God that he came and died for you himself. God gave his life for you to live a good and godly life with a secure eternity. You are worthy of being loved, adored, and cherished.

You are worth marrying a good and godly husband. You are worth being professed to, provided for, and protected by a man that sees you like Christ sees the Church. You are the righteousness of Christ. God favors you, and you have His eternal favor.

You are blessed with the blessings of Abraham, Isaac, and Jacob. God knows you and is waiting for you to come and meet with him. You are a purchased possession, and you belong to God himself. Men have left their seal on you, but in Christ, you have been sealed with the Holy Spirit, and He is here to help you.

You don't belong to any man who has not married you, but you belong to God. Because of everything you've been through, you might feel broken now, but in Christ, healing and wholeness are available. God wants you to be whole and heal, so allow him to heal you and make you whole.

You are a chosen woman in Christ. You are the apple of God's eyes, and God created you beautifully in his image. You are worth a man laying his hunt down because you are his special and good thing. You are a virtuous woman who is worth far more than rubies.

You are a precious crown that should be worn upon the head of your husband. YOU ARE A PRINCESS, DAUGHTER OF THE KING OF KINGS. My beloveth sister, when you know who you are and whose you are, you will not allow men to mistreat you. Because you know your worth, you will **NOT** put yourself on clearance. You know and understand that you are to choose the best husband for yourself.

Therefore, you will not allow Rayray, Pookie, Johnny, Ricky, or Zaddy to take you off the show floor and put you away on layaway, in the dark, in the corner, under the carpet where no one else can see you and find you. While in the meantime, the men who have you on layaway are still out there looking to find their one.

My beloveth, you now know that your body is the temple of God. That beautiful and glorious temple of King Solomon is representative of your body. Therefore, you will not allow men who have not paid the price to use your body. You now know that only your high priest that has gone through the process to profess his love, provide for you and protect you should have access to your body.

After reading *10 Years a Girlfriend*, you now understand that you should only have children in the bonds and covenant of marriage. Yes, our children outside of marriage are blessed. However, when we know better, we do better. Now that you've read 10 Years a Girlfriend, you know that you cannot force a man to love you.

You could pop out ten babies for him, but if he doesn't see you as Christ sees the church, nothing you do will cause him to love you independent of you. Take the time to come up with your husband list. What is it you desire in a husband? Come up with a plan to strategically place yourself in the right environment like Ruth did to meet her husband.

Finally, I admonish you to seek the face of the Lord about your husband. Perhaps, like me, your husband is held up in the spiritual realm. And you need to fast and pray for the Lord to give you the word of wisdom and knowledge you need.

You can read more about your identity in Chris in my In Christ I Am series.

About the Author

Janice is a wife to her wonderful husband, Michael Sr., and mom of two children born 20 years apart: Janice's beautiful and fashionable daughter, Alexia, and her inquisitive and joyful son, Michael Jr.

Janice loves to read and write. She writes passionately about subjects that mean the most to her. Additionally, Janice loves to tackle those "rock the boat" subjects.

Janice loves to spend time with her family, making their favorite meals, watching movies, enjoying a day at the park, shopping, doing girly stuff with Alexia, and playing and learning with her son Michael Jr.

Janice is the author of several books and has been writing for over 20 years. Her published books include:

1. Praying for Our Children
2. In Christ I Am
3. In Christ, I Am Prayer Journal
4. In Christ, I Am Bible Study Journal
5. Moments of Gratitude
6. The Phenomenon of Donald J Trump The GOP Nominee
7. The Naked Wife
8. 23 Types of Guys You Might Meet
9. 31 Days to NOT Being A Girlfriend If You Want to Be a Wife
10. How to Not Give Boyfriends Husband Benefits
11. 10 Years a Girlfriend

Additionally, Janice blogs @ www.janicehyltonblog.com

Connect with Janice on Facebook &

Instagram @ Author Janice Hylton
Facebook: Janice Hylton Blog and Author Janice Hylton
You can also connect with Janice on YouTube
Janice Hylton
Study the Bible in One Year
Allegedly Janice

www.ingramcontent.com/pod-product-compliance
Lightning Source LLC
Chambersburg PA
CBHW020852090426
42736CB00008B/346

* 9 7 8 1 9 4 6 2 4 2 1 3 6 *